SIXTH EDITION

FLASHMAPS
WASHINGTON DC

Editorial Updater
Patricia Fitzgerald

Cartographic Updater
Bello Design

Proofreader
Susan Gryder

Editor
Robert Blake

Cover Design
Guido Caroti

Creative Director
Fabrizio La Rocca

Cartographer
David Lindroth

Designer
Tigist Getachew

Cartographic Contributors
Edward Faherty
Tim Faherty
Page Lindroth
Dan Neumann
Eric Rudolph

Fodor's

www.fodors.com

Fodor's Travel Publications · New York, Toronto, London, Sydney, Auckland

Contents

ESSENTIAL INFORMATION	MAP
Important Telephone Numbers	iv–v
Washington DC Region	1
Washington DC/Baltimore Corridor	2
Washington DC Metropolitan Area	3
Neighborhoods	4
Streetfinder/Central Washington DC	5
Streetfinder/Upper Northwest	6
Zip Codes	7
Hospitals & Late-Night Pharmacies	8
Embassies	9
Universities, Colleges & Schools	10
Libraries	11

TRANSPORTATION	MAP
Airports	12
Area Metrorail System	13
Metrorail/Downtown	14
Driving/Metropolitan Area	15
Driving/Downtown	16
Buses/Downtown Washington	17
Buses/Arlington & Reagan National Airport	18
Buses/Northwest	19
Cab Zones	20

EXPLORING	MAP
Top Attractions	21
Exploring the Mall & Vicinity	22
The White House	23
United States Capitol	24
Museums	25
The Smithsonian Institution	26
National Gallery of Art/West Building	27
National Air & Space Museum	28
Exploring Georgetown	29
Churches, Temples & Mosques	30
Arlington Cemetery	31
Outdoor Statuary	32
Exploring Alexandria	33

PARKS & RECREATION   MAP

Parks 34
National Zoo 35
Rock Creek Park 36
National Arboretum 37
Biking Trails 38
Chesapeake & Ohio Canal 39
Great Falls Park 40
Stadiums & Arenas 41

SHOPPING   MAP

Shopping/Downtown 42
Shopping/Connecticut Avenue 43
Shopping/Georgetown 44
Area Shopping Centers 45

DINING & LODGING   MAP

Dining/Downtown 46
Dining/Capitol Hill & Waterfont 47
Dining/Georgetown 48
Dining/Northwest 49
Mall Lunch Spots 50
Dining/Metropolitan Area (with Alexandria) 51
Lodging/Downtown 52
Lodging/Metropolitan Area 53

NIGHTLIFE   MAP

Performing Arts 54
Kennedy Center 55
Movies 56
Nightlife/Washington 57
Nightlife/Georgetown 58

Special Sales

Fodor's Travel Publications are available at special discounts for bulk purchases for sales promotions or premiums. Special editions, including personalized covers, excerpts of existing guides, and corporate imprints, can be created in large quantities for special needs. For more information, contact your local bookseller or write to Special Markets, Fodor's Travel Publications, 1745 Broadway, New York, NY 10019. Inquiries from Canada should be directed to your local Canadian bookseller or sent to Random House of Canada, Ltd., Marketing Dept., 2775 Matheson Blvd. East, Mississauga, Ontario L4W 4P7. Inquiries from the United Kingdom should be sent to Fodor's Travel Publications, 20 Vauxhall Bridge Rd., London SW1V 2SA, England.   **ISBN 1-4000-1127-2**   **ISSN 1532-7221**

MANUFACTURED IN CHINA 10 9 8 7 6 5 4 3 2 1

Area Codes: DC (202); Maryland (301), (240), (410); Virginia (703), (571), (540).
All (202) unless otherwise noted.

EMERGENCIES

Ambulance, Fire, Police ☎ 911

AAA Emergency Road Service ☎ 703/222-5000

AMEX Lost Travelers Checks ☎ 800/221-7282

Animal Clinic ☎ 363-7300

Battered Women ☎ 347-2777

Children's Protection ☎ 671-SAFE

Deaf Emergency ☎ 911

Drug/Alcohol Hotline ☎ 800/821-4357

Gas Leaks ☎ 703/750-1000

Hazardous Wastes ☎ 911

Poison Control ☎ 625-3333

Police (non-emergency) ☎ 311

Power Outages ☎ 877-Pepco-62

Rape & Assault ☎ 333-7273

Suicide Prevention ☎ 561-7000

US Park Police ☎ 619-7300

SERVICES

AAA ☎ 703/222-6000

AIDS Hotline ☎ 332-2437

Alcoholics Anonymous ☎ 966-9115

American Red Cross ☎ 728-6400

Better Business Bureau ☎ 393-8000

Chamber of Commerce ☎ 347-7201

Crime Solvers ☎ 393-2222

DC Call Center ☎ 727-1000

Dominion Power ☎ 888/667-3000

Food Stamps ☎ 724-5506

Foreign Exchange Rates ☎ 800/287-7362

Immigration ☎ 800/375-5283

Legal Aid Society ☎ 628-1161

Mayor's Office ☎ 727-2980

Medicaid ☎ 639-4030

Medicare ☎ 800/633-4227

Motor Vehicle Information ☎ 727-5000

Office on Aging ☎ 724-5626

Passport Office ☎ 647-0518

Pepco ☎ 833-7500

Planned Parenthood ☎ 347-8500

Salvation Army ☎ 332-5000

Sanitation ☎ 727-1000

Social Security ☎ 800/772-1213

Social Services Information & Referral ☎ 463-6211

Special Olympics ☎ 408-2640

Supreme Court ☎ 479-3000

Time of Day ☎ 844-2525

Transportation for Handicapped ☎ 962-1245

US Capitol ☎ 224-3121

US Coast Guard ☎ 267-2229

US Customs Services ☎ 927-6724

US Internal Revenue ☎ 874-6748

US Postal Service ☎ 800/275-8777

Verizon ☎ 800/275-2355

Visitor Information ☎ 866/324-7386

Washington Convention & Tourism Corporation ☎ 789-7000

Washington DC Accommodations ☎ 289-2220; 800/554-2220

Washington Gas ☎ 800/752-7520.

Weather ☎ 936-1212

YMCA ☎ 232-6700

YWCA ☎ 626-0700

TRANSPORTATION

Amtrak ☎ 800/USA-RAIL

Baltimore-Washington International Airport ☎ 800/435-9294

Capitol Cab ☎ 546-2400

Diamond Cab ☎ 387-6200

Dulles International Airport ☎ 703/572-2700

Greyhound Bus Information ☎ 800/231-2222

Marc-Camden Line Commuter ☎ 800/325-7245

Marc-Penn Line Commuter ☎ 800/325-7245

Metrobus & Metrorail Transit Information ☎ 637-7000

Reagan Washington Nat'l Airport ☎ 703/417-8000

Super Shuttle ☎ 703/416-7873

Virginia Railway Express ☎ 703/684-0400

Washington Flyer ☎ 703/572-8400

Yellow Cab ☎ 544-1212

Area Codes: DC (202); Maryland (301), (240), (410); Virginia (703), (571), (540). All (202) unless otherwise noted.

TOURS

Black Educational Tours
☎ 301/248-6360

C&O Barge Trips ☎ 301/739-4200

Dandy Cruises ☎ 703/683-6076

DC Ducks ☎ 832-9800

FBI Tour ☎ 324-3447

Gold Line/Gray Line Tours
☎ 301/386-8300

National Cathedral ☎ 537-6200

Old Town Trolley Tours ☎ 301/985-3021

Pentagon Tour ☎ 703/697-1776

Scandal Tours ☎ 783-7212

Shore Shot ☎ 554-6500

Smithsonian Resident Associate Program ☎ 357-3030

Spirit of Washington ☎ 554-8000

Tourmobile ☎ 554-7950

UC Tours ☎ 554-4377

US Capitol ☎ 225-6857

Washington Post ☎ 334-7969

Washington Walks ☎ 484-1565

White House Tours ☎ 456-7041

PARKS AND RECREATION

Arlington National Cemetery
☎ 703/607-8000

Canoe Cruisers Hotline
☎ 301/656-2586

Cherry Blossom Festival ☎ 728-1137

C&O Canal Park Service ☎ 653-5190

DC Armory ☎ 547-9077

DC Freedom ☎ 547-3137

DC Parks & Recreation ☎ 673-7660

DC United ☎ 703/478-6600

Dial-A-Park ☎ 619-7275

FedEx Field ☎ 301/276-6000

Great Falls Visitor Center
☎ 703/285-2966

Laurel Race Park ☎ 301/725-0400

MCI Center ☎ 628-3200

National Aquarium ☎ 482-2825

National Arboretum ☎ 245-2726

National Botanical Garden
☎ 225-8333

National Park Service ☎ 208-4747

National Zoo ☎ 673-4800

Oriole Park at Camden Yards
☎ 410/685-9800

Patriot Center ☎ 703/993-3000

Road Runners Club ☎ 703/836-0558

RFK Stadium ☎ 547-9077

Rosecroft Raceway ☎ 301/567-4000

Washington Capitals ☎ 266-2350

Washington Mystics ☎ 661-5050

Washington Redskins ☎ 301/276-6000

Washington Wizards ☎ 661-5050

Wolf Trap Farm Park ☎ 703/255-1800

ENTERTAINMENT

Arena Stage ☎ 488-3300

Barns at Wolf Trap Park
☎ 703/938-2404

Choral Arts Society ☎ 244-3669

Constitution Hall ☎ 638-2661

Dial-A-Movie ☎ 333-3456

Dial-A-Museum ☎ 357-2020

Ford's Theatre ☎ 426-6924

Kennedy Center ☎ 467-4600

Lincoln Theater ☎ 328-6000

Lisner Auditorium ☎ 994-6800

Nat'l Symphony Orchestra ☎ 416-8100

National Theatre ☎ 628-6161

Nissan Pavilion ☎ 703/754-6400

Shakespeare Theatre at the Lansburgh ☎ 547-1122

Smithsonian Information ☎ 357-2700

Studio Theatre ☎ 332-3300

Ticket Place ☎ 842-5387

Ticketmaster ☎ 432-7328

Warner Theater ☎ 783-4000

Washington Ballet ☎ 362-3606

Washington Chorus ☎ 342-6221

Washington Opera ☎ 800/87-OPERA

Wolf Trap ☎ 703/255-1800

SALES TAX

Washington, DC: 5.75%

Maryland: 5%

Virginia: 4.5%

MAP 2

Washington DC/Baltimore Corridor

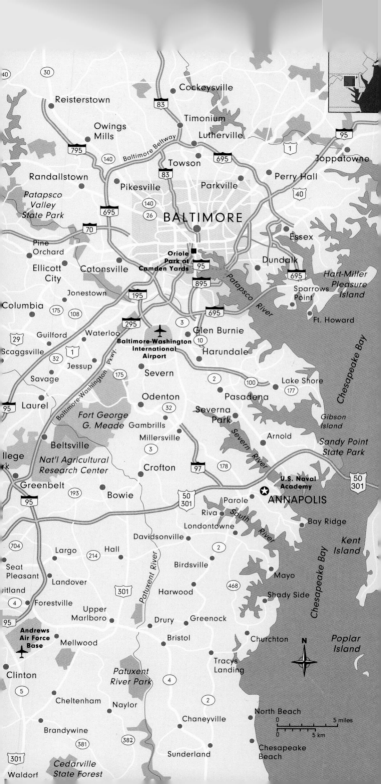

MARYLAND

Kensington

University Blvd.

Georgia Ave.

270

270

495

189

River Rd.

Old Georgetown Rd.

Wisconsin Ave.

495

Falls Rd.

190

Persimmon Tree Rd.

191

Bradley Blvd.

191

Bradley Blvd.

187

355

185

Connecticut Ave.

Wilson La.

Bethesda

Glen Echo

MacArthur Blvd.

Goldsboro Rd.

Somerset

Bradley La.

Beach Dr.

Oregon Ave.

Utah Ave.

Chevy Chase

River Rd.

396

Military Rd.

Rock Creek Park

193

American Legion Br.

Potomac River

495

Georgetown Pike

Langley

George Washington Memorial Pkwy.

MARYLAND
DISTRICT OF COLUMBIA

Massachusetts Ave.

Wisconsin Ave.

Connecticut Ave.

National Zoological Park

Dulles Int'l Airport

267

Tysons Corner

Maple Ave.

Dolley Madison Blvd.

McLean

Old Dominion Dr.

Dulles Airport Access Rd.

Westmoreland St.

Kirby Rd.

N. Glebe Rd.

Military Rd.

Canal Rd.

MacArthur Blvd.

Calvert St.

C&O Canal

Gallows Rd.

Curtis Memorial Pkwy.

Williamsburg Blvd.

Glebe Rd.

Lee Hwy.

29

Washington Blvd.

Lee Hwy.

Roosevelt Island

New Hampshire

NW N NE
W   E
SW S SE

Falls Church

Leesburg Pike

66

7

Lee Hwy.

Arlington Blvd.

50

Wilson Blvd.

Arlington

Arlington National Cemetery

495

Capital Beltway

Gallows Rd.

Hummer Rd.

Annandale Rd.

Sleepy Hollow Rd.

Leesburg Pike

Arlington Blvd.

George Mason Dr.

Glebe Rd.

Columbia Pike

Jefferson Davis Hwy.

George Washington

Columbia Pike

VIRGINIA

Annandale

236

Little River Tnpk.

Backlick Rd.

Seminary Rd.

395

King St.

Van Dorn St.

Henry G. Shirley Memorial Hwy.

Quaker Ln.

Glebe Rd.

Mt. Vernon Ave.

Braddock Rd.

King St.

Alexandria

1

Braddock Rd.

Duke St.

7

236

95

495

617

95

Old Keene Mill Rd.

Backlick Rd.

Hooes Rd.

Beulah St.

Capital Beltway

Franconia Rd.

Telegraph Rd.

South Kings Hwy.

Richmond Hwy.

Fort Hunt Rd.

1

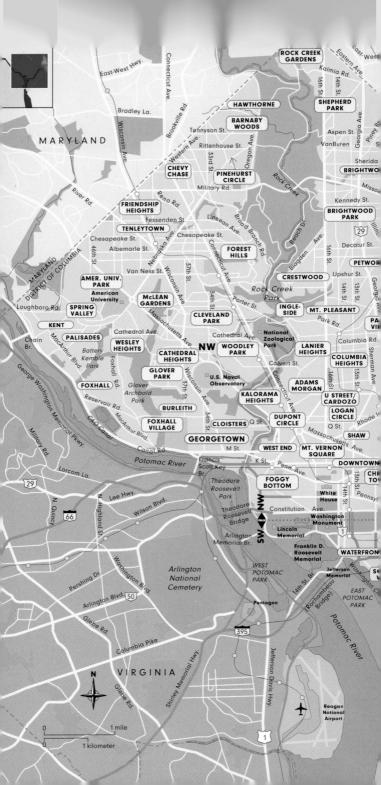

MAP 3
Street Finder/Central Washington DC

MAP 5 | Street Finder/Central Washington DC

Numbers refer to grid locations on map

Adams St. E1, F1
Ashmead Pl. C1
Avon La. A2
Avon Pl. A2
Bancroft Pl. B2, C2
Barry Pl. D1, E1
Bates St. E2, F2
Belmont Rd. C1
Belmont St. C1, D1
Benton Pl. B1
Biltmore St. C1
Bryant St. E1, F1
C St. NW, NE B4, F4
C St. SW, SE D5, F5
California St. B1, C1
Calvert St. B1, C1
Cambridge Pl. B2
Canal St. E5, F6
Caroline St. D1
Carrollburg Pl. F6
Champlain St. C1
Channing St. F1
Chapin St. D1
Church St. C2, D2
Cleveland Ave. A1, B1
Clifton St. D1
College St. E1
Columbia Rd. C1, D1
Connecticut Ave. B1, C3
Constitution Ave. B4, F4
Corcoran St. C2, D2
Crescent Pl. C1
Cushing Pl. F6
D St. NW, NE C4, F4
D St. SW, SE D5, F5
Decatur Pl. B2, C2
Delaware Ave. F4
Dent Pl. A2, B2
DeSales St. C3
Duddington Pl. F5
Dumbarton St. A2, B2
Dupont Circle C2
E St. NW, NE B4, F4
E St. SW, SE E5, F5
East Basin Dr. D5
East Capitol St. F4
Eckington Pl. F2
Edgevale Terr. B1
Ellipse Rd. C4, D4
Elm St. E1
Euclid St. C1, D1
F St. NW, NE B4, F4
F St. SE F5

Fairmont St. D1
Flagler Pl. E1
Florida Ave. C2, F2
French St. D2, E2
Fuller St. D1
G St. NW, NE B3, F3
G St. SW, SE D5, F5
George Washington Memorial Pkwy. A3, C6
Georgia Ave. E1
Girard St. D1, F1
Grace St. A3
H St. NW, NE B3, F3
H St. SW, SE E5, F5
Half St. SE F6
Half St. SW F6
Hall Pl. A1
Harvard St. C1, E1
Hawthorne Ave. B1
Henry Bacon Dr. C4
Hobart St. C1
Howard Pl. E1
Howison Pl. F6
I St. NW, NE B3, F3
I St. SW, SE E6, F6
Independence Ave. B5, F5
Indiana Ave. E4
Ivy St. F5
Jackson Pl. C3
Jefferson Dr. D5, E5
Jefferson Pl. C3
Johnson Ave. D2
K St. NW, NE B3, F3
K St. SW, SE E6, F6
Kalorama Circle B1
Kalorama Rd. B1, C1
L St. NW, NE B3, F3
L St. SW, SE E6, F6
Lanier Pl. C1
Lincoln Rd. F1, F2
Logan Circle D2
Louisiana Ave. F4
M St. NW, NE A3, F3
M St. SW, SE E6, F6
Madison Dr. D4, E4
Madison Pl. D3
Maine Ave. D5, E6
Makamie Pl. E6
Market Pl. E4
Maryland Ave. E5, F4
Massachusetts Ave. A1, F3
McGill Terr. B1

McMillan Dr. E1
Memorial Dr. A5, B5
Michigan Ave. E1, F1
Mintwood Rd. C1
Mt. Vernon Sq. E3
N St. NW, NE A3, F2
N St. SW, SE E6, F6
Neal Pl. E2
New Hampshire Ave. B4, D1
New Jersey Ave. E2, F6
New York Ave. C4, F2
Newport Pl. C2
Normanstone Dr. A1, B1
North Capitol St. F1, F4
O St. NW, NE A2, F2
O St. SW, SE E6, F6
Observatory Circle A1
Observatory La. A1
Ohio Dr. C5
Olive St. B3
Ontario Rd. C1
P St. NW, NE A2, F2
Patterson St. F3
Pennsylvania Ave. B3, E4
Pierce St. F3
Potomac St. A2, A3
Prospect St. A3
Q St. A2, F2
Quincy Pl. F2
R St. NW, NE A2, F2
Randolph Pl. E2, F2
Reservoir Rd. A2
Rhode Island Ave. C3, F1
Riggs Pl. C2, D2
Rock Creek & Potomac Pkwy. B1, B4
Rock Creek Dr. B1
S St. NW, NE A2, F2
School St. E5
Scott Circle C2, D2
Seaton Pl. C1, F2
Seaton St. C1
Sheridan Circle B2
Sherman Ave. D1
Shoreham Dr. B1
South St. A3
South Capitol St. F5, F6
South Executive Pl. C4, D4
State Pl. C4
Summit St. F1

A · B · C

Kirke St.
Irving St.

Rittenhouse St.
Quesada St.
Patterson Pl.
Patterson St.

Magnolia Pkwy.
Cedar Pkwy.
Grafton St.
Chevy Chase Circle
Oliver St.
Oliver St.
Oliver St.
Northampton St.
Northampton St.

Nebraska
33rd St.
32nd St.
30th St.
30th St.

Park St.
Center St.
Grove St.
Kirkside Dr.
Montgomery St.
Belt Rd.
Western Ave.

McKinley St.
Chevy Chase Pkwy.
Nevada Ave.
Broad Branch Rd.

Legation St.
31st St.

Newla
Par

1
Wisconsin Ave.
The Hills Plaza
Wisconsin Circle
Willard Ave.

Morrison St.
Livingston St.
Legation St.

Military Rd.
Military Rd.
Military Rd.

MARYLAND
DISTRICT OF COLUMBIA

Kanawha St.
Jocelyn St.
Jenifer St.
Ingomar St.

Nebraska Ave.
32nd St.

R
Cr
P

Hills Plaza
42nd Pl.
Belts La.
Bell Rd.
41st St.
Reno Rd.

Jenifer St.
Reno Rd.
39th St.
38th St.

Linnean Terr.
Broad Branch Rd.
34th St.
33rd St.

Branch Rd.

2
Harrison St.
Garrison St.
Faraday Pl.

43rd St.
42nd St.

Ingomar St.
Huntington St.
Harrison St.
Gramercy St.
Garrison St.
Fessenden St.

Chevy Chase Pkwy.
Everett St.

Garrison St.
Fessen St.
Linnean Ave.

River Rd.
44th St.
45th St.
43rd St.
43rd St.
Ellicott St.

Emory Pl.
Donaldson Pl.
De Bussey St.
Howard St.

Ellicott St.

Fort Reno Park

Fort Reno Pumping Station

Davenport St.
Chespeake St.
Brandywine St.
Murdock Mill Rd.
Albemarle St.

43rd Pl.
Butterworth Pl.

Grant Rd.

Davenport St.
Cumberland St.
Chesapeake St.
Brandywine St.
Appleton St.

Nebraska Rd.
38th St.
36th St.

Connecticut Ave.
32nd St.

Davenport St.
Grant Rd.
Gates Rd.
Brandywine St.
31st St.
Albemarle St.

29

3
Alton Pl.
Yuma St.
Windom Pl.
Warren St.
Verplanck Pl.

43rd St.

Grant Rd.
Tenley Circle
40th St.
Alton Pl.
Yuma St.
Windom Pl.
39th St.
37th St.
Reno Rd.

Veazey St.

University of the District of Columbia

Audubon Terr.
Sunshine Va
Park

Veazey Terr.
35th St.

Howa
University
Scho

Van Ness St.
41st St.

Van Ness St.
Upton St.
Tilden St.

Van Ness St.
Connecticut Ave.
Upton St.
Tilden S

4
45th St.
Tindall St.
Springdale St.
Sedgwick St.
44th St.
Nebraska Ave.

Wisconsin Ave.

Upton St.
Tilden St.
Sidwell Friends School
Rodman St.
Rodman St.
Quebec St.
Porter St.
Ordway St.

SpringLand La.
35th St.

Tilden St.
Melvin Park
Sedgwick St.
Rowland
Quebec St.
34th St.
33rd St.
Porter St.
30th St.

Department of Homeland Security

Ward Circle

American University

Porter St.

Glover Archbold Park

Newark St.
Macomb St.
Lowell St.
35th Pl.
34th St.
Highland Pl.
34th St.
Ashley Terr.

Newark St.
5
Macomb St.
Lowell St.
Klingle St.
Cathedral Ave.
Hawthorne St.
Garfield St.

New Mexico Ave.
Embassy Park Dr.
Sutton Pl.
43rd St.
45th Pl.
45th St.
43rd Pl.

West
Idaho Ave.
Massachusetts Ave.
38th St.
Klingle Pl.
39th St.
Bellevue Terr.

Macomb St.
Lowell St.
Woodley Rd.

Washington National Cathedral

Garfield

36th Pl.
36th St.
35th Pl.
35th St.

34th St.
33rd St.
Woodley Rd.
Klingle Rd.
Cortla
Cathedral Ave
Hawthorne St.

32nd St.
31st St.
Klingle Rd.

Baxter
Garfield St.

6
Edmunds St.
Dexter St.

Foxhall Rd.

Glover Archbold Park

N

Tunlaw Terr.
42nd St.
41st St.
40th St.
Edmunds St.
Davis Pl.
Calvert St.
39th St.
40th St.
Beecher
Benton St.

Tunlaw Rd.
Garrett St.
Huidekoper Pl.
38th St.
Watson Pl.
Fulton St.
Davis Pl.
38th Pl.
Observatory Pl.

Wisconsin Ave.
35th St.
Nor
34th St.

Cleveland Ave.
Woodland Dr.
31st St.
32nd St.
Normanstone Terr.

Garfield St.
Woodley Rd.
Cathedral Ave
Hawthorne St.
31st St.

Circle
Observatory Circle
Naval Observatory
Observatory La.
Hall Pl.

0 —— 1200 feet
0 —— 400 meters

A · B · C

Numbers refer to grid locations on map

Albemarle Rd. A3, C3
Alton Pl. A3, C3
Appleton St. B3, C3
Ashley Terr. C4
Audubon Terr. C3
Baxter St. C5
Beecher A6, B6
Belt Rd. A2, B3
Benton St. B6
Branch Rd. C2
Brandywine St. A3, C3
Broad Branch Rd. B1, C2
Broad Branch Terr. C2
Calvert St. B6
Cathedral Ave. A5, C5
Cedar Pkwy. A1
Center St. A1
Chesapeake St. A3, C3
Chevy Chase Circle B1
Chevy Chase Pkwy. B1, B2
Cleveland Ave. C5, C6
Connecticut Ave. B1, C5
Cortland Pl. C5
Cumberland St. B3, C3
Davenport St. A3, C3
Davis Pl. B6
Davis St. B6
DeBussey St. B3
Dexter St. A6
Donaldson Pl. B2, B3
Edmunds St. A6, B6
Ellicott St. A2, C2
Embassy Park Dr. A5
Emory Pl. A2, B2
Faraday Pl. A2
Fessenden St. A2, C2
Foxhall Rd. A5, A6
Fulton St. A6, C6
Garfield St. A5, C5
Garfield Terr. C6
Garrison St. A2, C2
Gates Rd. C3
Grafton St. A1, B1
Gramercy St. B2
Grant Rd. B3
Grove St. A1
Hall Pl. B6
Harrison St. A2, B2
Hawthorne St. A5, C5
Highland Pl. C5
Huidekoper Pl. B6

Huntington St. B2
Idaho Ave. B4, B5
Ingomar St. A2, B2
Irving St. A1, B1
Jenifer St. A2, C2
Jocelyn St. B2, C2
Kanawha St. B2
Kirke St. A1, B1
Kirkside Dr. A1
Klingle Pl. B5
Klingle Rd. C5
Klingle St. A5
Legation St. A1, C1
Linnean Ave. C2
Linnean Terr. C2
Livingston St. A1, C1
Lowell St. A5, C5
Macomb St. A5, C5
Magnolia Pkwy. A1, B1
Massachusetts Ave. A4, C6
McKinley St. B1, C1
Military Rd. A1, C1
Montgomery St. A1
Morrison St. A1, C1
Murdock Mill Rd. A3
Nebraska Ave. A5, C1
Nevada Ave. B1
New Mexico Ave. A5, A6
Newark St. A5, C5
Normanstone La. C5, C6
Normanstone Terr. C6
Northampton St. B1, C1
Observatory Circle B6, C6
Observatory La. B6, C6
Observatory Pl. B6
Oliver St. A1, C1
Ordway St. B4, C4
Park St. A1
Patterson Pl. C1
Patterson St. B1, C1
Porter St. B4, C4
Quesada St. B1, C1
Quebec St. B4, C4
Reno Rd. B2, C4
Rittenhouse St. B1, C1
River Rd. A2, A3
Rodman St. B4, C4
Rowland Pl. C4
Sedgwick St. A4, C4

Springdale St. A4
Springland La. B4, C4
Tenley Circle B3
The Hills Plaza A1
Tilden St. B4, C4
Tindall St. A4
Tunlaw Rd. B6
Tunlaw Terr. B6
Upton St. B4, C4
Van Ness St. A4, C4
Veazey St. B3
Veazey Terr. C3
Verplanck Pl. A4
Ward Circle A4
Warren St. A3, C3
Watson Pl. B6
Western Ave. A2, B1
Westover Pl. A4, A5
Willard Ave. A1
Windom Pl. A3, B3
Wisconsin Ave. A1, B6
Woodland Dr. C6
Woodley Rd. B5, C5
Yuma St. A3, C3
29th Pl. C3, C6
29th St. C3
30th Pl. C1, C2
30th St. C1, C6
31st Pl. C6
31st St. C1, C6
32nd St. C1, C6
33rd St. C1, C5
34th Pl. C6
34th St. C2, C6
35th Pl. B6
35th St. C3, C6
36th Pl. B6
36th St. B2, B6
37th St. B3, B4
38th St. B1, B5
39th Pl. B6
39th St. B1, B6
40th Pl. B6
40th St. B3, B6
41st St. B1, A6
42nd St. A1, A6
43rd Pl. A2, A3
43rd St. A2, A5
44th St. A2, A6
45th Pl. A5
45th St. A2, A5

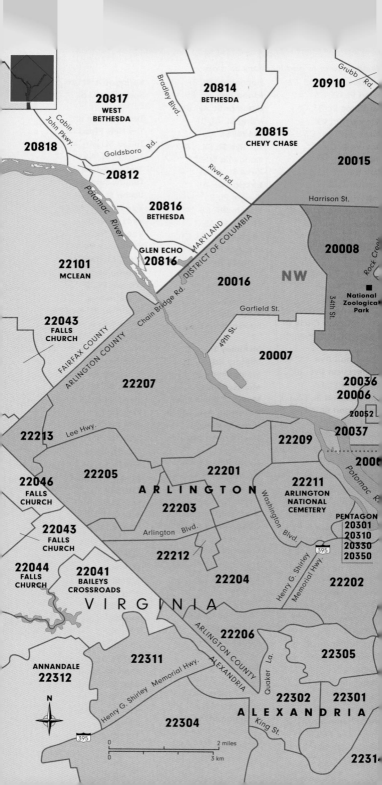

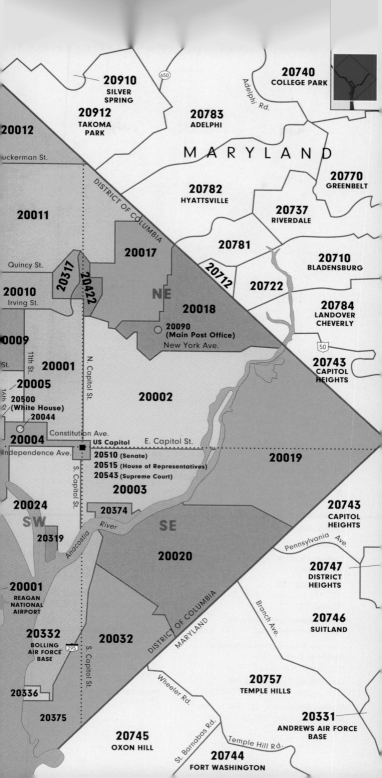

MAP 8
Hospitals & Late-Night Pharmacies

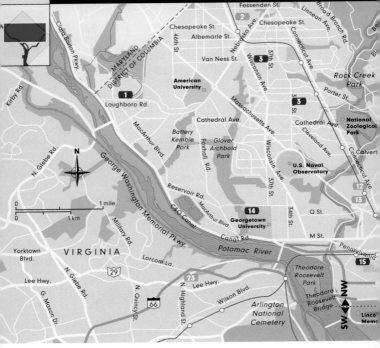

Listed by Site Number

1 Sibley Memorial
2 CVS Drug Stores
3 Psychiatric Institute of DC
4 Walter Reed Army Medical Center
5 Providence
6 Hospital for Sick Children
7 Veterans Affairs Medical Center
8 National Rehabilitation
9 Children's
10 Washington Hospital Center
11 Howard University
12 Rite-Aid Pharmacy
13 CVS Drug Stores
14 Georgetown University

Listed Alphabetically

HOSPITALS

Children's, 9. 111 Michigan Ave NW
☎ 884–5000

DC General, 18.
1900 Massachusetts Ave SE
☎ 698–5000

Georgetown University, 14.
3800 Reservoir Rd NW ☎ 444–2000

George Washington University Medical Center, 15.
901 23rd St NW ☎ 715–4000

Greater SE Community, 20.
1310 Southern Ave SE ☎ 574–6000

Hadley Memorial, 21. 4601 Martin Luther King Jr Ave SW ☎ 574–5700

Hospital for Sick Children, 6.
1731 Bunker Hill Rd NE ☎ 832–4400

Howard University, 11.
2041 Georgia Ave NW ☎ 865–6100

Medlink Hospital and Nursing Center at Capitol Hill, 17.
700 Constitution Ave NE ☎ 546–5700

National Rehabilitation, 8.
102 Irving St NW ☎ 877–1000

Prince George's Hospital Center, 22
3001 Hospital Dr, Cheverly, MD
☎ 301/618–2000

Providence, 5. 1150 Varnum St NE
☎ 269–7000

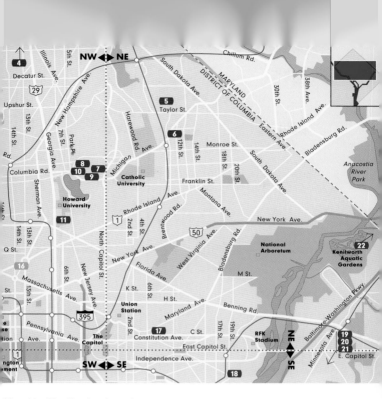

Listed by Site Number (cont.)

15 George Washington University Medical Center

16 CVS Drug Stores

17 Medlink Hospital and Nursing Center at Capitol Hill

18 DC General

19 St Elizabeth's

20 Greater SE Community

21 Hadley Memorial

22 Prince George's Hospital Center

23 CVS Drug Stores

Listed Alphabetically (cont.)

Psychiatric Institute of DC, 3.
4228 Wisconsin Ave NW ☎ 965–8200

Sibley Memorial, 1.
5255 Loughboro Rd NW ☎ 537–4000

St Elizabeths, 19. 2700 Martin Luther King Jr Ave SE ☎ 562–4000

Veterans Affairs Medical Center, 7.
50 Irving St NW ☎ 745–8000

Walter Reed Army Medical Center, 4.
6900 Georgia Ave NW ☎ 782–3501

Washington Hospital Center, 10.
110 Irving St NW ☎ 877–7000

LATE-NIGHT/24-HOUR PHARMACIES

CVS Drug Stores, 2.
4555 Wisconsin Ave NW ☎ 537–1587

CVS Drug Stores, 13.
6-7 Dupont Circle NW ☎ 785–1466

CVS Drug Stores, 16.
1199 Vermont Ave NW ☎ 628–0720

CVS Drug Stores, 23.
3133 Lee Hwy Arlington, VA
☎ 703/522–0260

Rite-Aid Pharmacy, 12.
1815 Connecticut Ave NW ☎ 332–1718

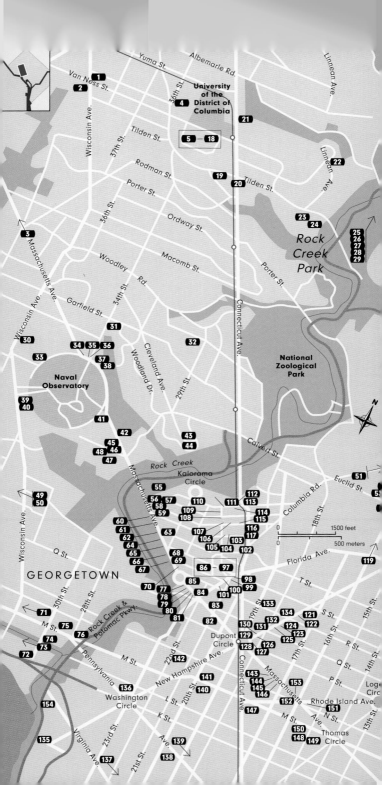

Listed Alphabetically

Albania, 92. 2100 S St NW
☎ 223-4942

Algeria, 114. 2137 Wyoming Ave NW
☎ 265-2800

Angola, 54. 2100-2108 16th St NW
☎ 785-1156

Argentina, 131. 1600 New Hampshire
Ave NW ☎ 238-6400

Armenia, 94. 2225 R St NW
☎ 319-1976

Australia, 153. 1601 Massachusetts
Ave NW ☎ 797-3000

Austria, 4. 3524 International Ct NW
☎ 895-6700

Azerbaijan, 36. 2741 34th St NW
☎ 337-3500

Bahamas, 78. 2220 Massachusetts
Ave NW ☎ 319-2660

Bahrain, 12. 3502 International Dr
NW ☎ 342-1111

Bangladesh, 15. 3510 International
Dr NW ☎ 244-0183

Barbados, 106. 2144 Wyoming Ave
NW ☎ 939-9200

Belarus, 123. 1619 New Hampshire
Ave NW ☎ 986-1606

Belgium, 31. 3330 Garfield St NW
☎ 333-6900

Belize, 56. 2535 Massachusetts Ave
NW ☎ 332-9636

Benin, 113. 2124 Kalorama Rd NW
☎ 232-6656

Bolivia, 45. 3014 Massachusetts Ave
NW ☎ 483-4410

Bosnia/Herzegovina, 137.
2109 E St NW ☎ 337-1500

Botswana, 130. 1531-3 New
Hampshire Ave NW ☎ 244-4990

Brazil, 46. 3006 Massachusetts Ave
NW ☎ 238-2700

Brunei, 8. 3520 International Ct NW
☎ 237-1838

Bulgaria, 87. 1621 22nd St NW
☎ 387-0174

Burkina Faso, 67. 2340 Massachusetts
Ave NW ☎ 332-5577

Burundi, 39. 2233 Wisconsin Ave NW
☎ 342-2574

Cambodia, 29. 4530 16th St NW
☎ 726-7742

Cameroon, 68.
2349 Massachusetts Ave NW
☎ 265-8790

Canada, 139. 501 Pennsylvania
Ave NW ☎ 682-1740

Cape Verde, 34. 3415
Massachusetts Ave NW ☎ 965-6820

Central African Republic, 86.
1618 22nd St NW ☎ 483-7800

Chad, 98. 2002 R St NW ☎ 462-4009

Chile, 144. 1732 Massachusetts Ave
NW ☎ 785-1746

China (People's Republic), 112. 2300
Connecticut Ave NW ☎ 328-2500

Colombia, 103. 2118 Leroy Pl NW
☎ 387-8338

Congo, 25. 4891 Colorado Ave NW
☎ 726-5500

Costa Rica, 91. 2114 S St NW
☎ 234-2945

Cote d'Ivoire, 62. 2424 Massachusetts
Ave NW ☎ 797-0300

Croatia, 69. 2343 Massachusetts Ave
NW ☎ 588-5899

Cuban Interests Section, 52.
2630 16th St NW ☎ 797-8518

Cyprus, 96. 2211 R St NW ☎ 462-5772

Czech Republic, 24. 3900 Spring of
Freedom St NW ☎ 274-9100

**Democratic Republic of Congo
(formerly Zaire), 120.** 1800 New
Hampshire Ave NW ☎ 234-7960

Denmark, 48. 3200 Whitehaven St NW
☎ 234-4300

Djibouti, 148. 1156 15th St NW
☎ 331-0270

Dominican Republic, 88.
1715 22nd St NW ☎ 332-6280

Ecuador, 119. 2535 15th St NW
☎ 234-7200

Egypt, 9. 3521 International Ct NW
☎ 895-5400

El Salvador, 109. 2308 California St
NW ☎ 265-9671

Eritrea, 122. 1708 New Hampshire
Ave NW ☎ 319-1991

Estonia, 147. 1730 M St NW
☎ 588-0101

Ethiopia, 14. 3506 International Dr
NW ☎ 234-1200

Fiji, 39. 2233 Wisconsin Ave NW
☎ 337-8320

Finland, 38. 3301 Massachusetts Ave
NW ☎ 298-5800

France, 50. 4101 Reservoir Rd NW
☎ 944-6000

Listed Alphabetically (cont.)

Gabon, 116. 2034 20th St NW
☎ 797-1000

Gambia, 149. 1155 15th St NW
☎ 785-1399

Georgia Republic, 128. 1615 New Hampshire Ave NW ☎ 387-2390

Germany, 49. 4645 Reservoir Rd NW
☎ 298-4000

Ghana, 16. 3512 International Dr NW
☎ 686-4520

Great Britain, 41. 3100 Massachusetts Ave NW ☎ 588-6500

Greece, 85. 2221 Massachusetts Ave NW ☎ 939-5800

Grenada, 134. 1701 New Hampshire Ave NW ☎ 265-2561

Guatemala, 95. 2220 R St NW
☎ 745-4952

Guinea, 117. 2112 Leroy Pl NW
☎ 483-9420

Guyana, 57. 2490 Tracy Pl NW
☎ 265-6900

Haiti, 70. 2311 Massachusetts Ave NW ☎ 332-4090

Honduras, 19. 3007 Tilden St NW
☎ 966-7702

Hungary, 23. 3910 Shoemaker St NW
☎ 362-6730

Iceland, 148. 1156 15th St NW
☎ 265-6653

India, 83. 2107 Massachusetts Ave NW
☎ 939-7000

Indonesia, 127. 2020 Massachusetts Ave NW ☎ 775-5200

Iranian Interests Section, 40.
2209 Wisconsin Ave NW ☎ 965-4990

Iraqi Interests Section, 82.
1801 P St NW ☎ 483-7500

Ireland, 77. 2234 Massachusetts Ave NW ☎ 462-3939

Israel, 17. 3514 International Dr NW
☎ 364-5500

Italy, 47. 3000 Whitehaven St NW
☎ 612-4400

Jamaica, 126. 1520 New Hampshire Ave NW ☎ 452-0660

Japan, 60. 2520 Massachusetts Ave NW ☎ 238-6700

Jordan, 13. 3504 International Dr NW
☎ 966-2664

Kenya, 93. 2249 R St NW ☎ 387-6101

Korea, 61. 2450 Massachusetts Ave NW ☎ 939-5600

Kuwait, 20. 2940 Tilden St NW
☎ 966-0702

Laos, 90. 2222 S St NW ☎ 332-6416

Latvia, 26. 4325 17th St NW
☎ 726-8213

Lebanon, 44. 2560 28th St NW
☎ 939-6300

Lesotho, 59. 2511 Massachusetts Ave NW ☎ 797-5533

Liberia, 28. 5201 16th St NW
☎ 723-0437

Lithuania, 53. 2622 16th St NW
☎ 234-5860

Luxembourg, 81. 2200 Massachusetts Ave NW ☎ 265-4171

Macedonia, 72. 3050 K St NW
☎ 337-3063

Madagascar, 66. 2374 Massachusetts Ave NW ☎ 265-5525

Malawi, 64. 2408 Massachusetts Ave NW ☎ 797-1007

Malaysia, 5. 3516 International Ct NW ☎ 572-9700

Mali, 101. 2130 R St NW ☎ 332-2249

Malta, 102. 2017 Connecticut Ave NW
☎ 462-3611

Mauritania, 104. 2129 Leroy Pl NW
☎ 232-5700

Mauritius, 21. 4301 Connecticut Ave NW ☎ 244-1491

Mexico, 138. 1911 Pennsylvania Ave NW ☎ 728-1600

Mongolia, 75. 2833 M St NW
☎ 333-7117

Morocco, 100. 1601 21st St NW
☎ 462-7979

Mozambique, 140. 1990 M St NW
☎ 293-7146

Myanmar, 89. 2300 S St NW
☎ 332-9044

Namibia, 125. 1605 New Hampshire Ave NW ☎ 986-0540

Nepal, 105. 2131 Leroy Pl NW
☎ 667-4550

Netherlands, 22.
4200 Linnean Ave NW ☎ 244-5300

New Zealand, 33. 37 Observatory Circle NW ☎ 328-4800

Nicaragua, 124. 1627 New Hampshire Ave NW ☎ 939-6570

Niger, 97. 2204 R St NW ☎ 483-4224

Listed Alphabetically (cont.)

Nigeria, 7. 3519 International Ct NW
☎ 986-8400

Norway, 35. 2720 34th St NW
☎ 333-6000

Oman, 55. 2535 Belmont Rd NW
☎ 387-1980

Pakistan, 6. 3517 International Ct NW
☎ 243-6500

Panama, 43. 2862 McGill Ter NW
☎ 483-1407

Paraguay, 65. 2400 Massachusetts
Ave NW ☎ 483-6960

Peru, 146. 1700 Massachusetts Ave
NW ☎ 833-9860

Philippines, 152. 1600 Massachusetts
Ave NW ☎ 467-9300

Poland, 51. 2640 16th St NW
☎ 234-3800

Portugal, 111. 2125 Kalorama Rd NW
☎ 328-8610

Qatar, 2. 4200 Wisconsin Ave NW
☎ 274-1600

Romania, 84. 1607 23rd St NW
☎ 332-4846

Russia, 30. 2650 Wisconsin Ave NW
☎ 298-5700

Rwanda, 121. 1714 New Hampshire
Ave NW ☎ 232-2882

Saudi Arabia, 135. 601 New
Hampshire Ave NW ☎ 337-4076

Senegal, 115. 2112 Wyoming Ave NW
☎ 234-0540

Sierra Leone, 133. 1701 19th St NW
☎ 939-9261

Singapore, 18. 3501 International Pl
NW ☎ 537-3100

Slovak Republic, 10.
3523 International Ct NW ☎ 237-1054

Slovenia, 129. 1525 New Hampshire
Ave NW ☎ 667-5363

South Africa, 42. 3051 Massachusetts
Ave NW ☎ 232-4400

Spain, 136. 2375 Pennsylvania Ave NW
☎ 452-0100

Sri Lanka, 107. 2148 Wyoming Ave NW
☎ 483-4025

St. Kitts and Nevis, 3. 3216 New
Mexico Ave NW ☎ 686-2636

St Lucia, 3. 3216 New Mexico Ave
NW ☎ 364-6792

St. Vincent and The Grenadines, 3.
3216 New Mexico Ave NW
☎ 364-6730

Sudan, 79. 2210 Massachusetts
Ave NW ☎ 338-8565

Suriname, 15. 4301 Connecticut
Ave NW ☎ 244-7488

Swaziland, 11. 3400 International Dr
NW ☎ 362-6683

Sweden, 150. 1501 M St NW
☎ 467-2600

Switzerland, 32. 2900 Cathedral Ave
NW ☎ 745-7900

Syria, 108. 2215 Wyoming Ave NW
☎ 232-6313

Taiwan, Republic of China, 1.
4201 Wisconsin Ave NW ☎ 895-1800

Tanzania, 99. 2139 R St NW
☎ 939-6125

Thailand, 73. 1024 Wisconsin Ave NW
☎ 944-3600

Togo, 80. 2208 Massachusetts Ave
NW ☎ 234-4212

Trinidad & Tobago, 145. 1708
Massachusetts Ave NW ☎ 467-6490

Tunisia, 151. 1515 Massachusetts Ave
NW ☎ 862-1850

Turkey, 58. 2525 Massachusetts Ave
NW ☎ 612-6700

Uganda, 27 5911 16th St NW
☎ 726-7100

Ukraine, 71. 3350 M St NW
☎ 333-0606

United Arab Emirates, 142.
1255 22nd St NW ☎ 243-2400

Uruguay, 76. 2715 M St NW
☎ 331-1313

Uzbekistan, 143. 1746 Massachusetts
Ave NW ☎ 887-5300

Vatican/Holy See, 37. 3339
Massachusetts Ave NW ☎ 333-7121

Venezuela, 74. 1099 30th St NW
☎ 342-2214

Vietnam, 141. 1233 20th St NW
☎ 861-0737

Yemen, 154. 2600 Virginia Ave NW
☎ 965-4760

Yugoslavia, 110. 2410 California St
NW ☎ 332-0333

Zambia, 63. 2419 Massachusetts Ave
NW ☎ 265-9717

Zimbabwe, 132. 1608 New
Hampshire Ave NW ☎ 332-7100

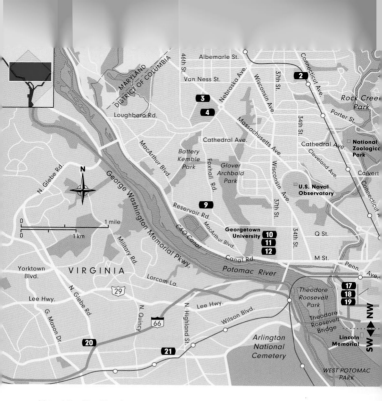

Listed by Site Number

1   University of
    Maryland, University
    College

2   University of DC

3   Wesley Theological
    Seminary

4   American University

5   Catholic University of
    America

6   Trinity College

7   St Paul's College

8   Howard University

9   Mt Vernon College

10 Georgetown
    University

11 Georgetown School
    of Nursing

12 Georgetown School
    of Medicine

13 Johns Hopkins Univ,
    Nitze School of
    Advanced
    International Studies

Listed Alphabetically

American University, 4.
4400 Massachusetts Ave NW
☎ 885-1000

Catholic University of America, 5.
620 Michigan Ave NE ☎ 319-5000

**Department of Agriculture
Graduate School, 22.**
600 Maryland Ave SW
☎ 888/744-4723

Gallaudet University, 14.
800 Florida Ave NE ☎ 651-5000

**George Mason Arlington Campus,
21.** 3401 N Fairfax Dr, Arlington VA
☎ 703/993-8999

George Washington University, 17.
2121 I St NW ☎ 994-1000

**George Washington University
Law School, 19.** 2000 H St NW
☎ 994-1000

**George Washington University
School of Medicine, 18.**
2300 I St NW ☎ 994-2987

**Georgetown University Law Center,
16.** 600 New Jersey Ave NW
☎ 662-9000

**Georgetown University Medical
Center School of Medicine, 12.**
3900 Reservoir Rd NW ☎ 687-1154

**Georgetown University Medical
Center School of Nursing, 11.**
3700 Reservoir Rd NW ☎ 687-0100

Georgetown University, 10.
O & 37th Sts NW ☎ 687-0100

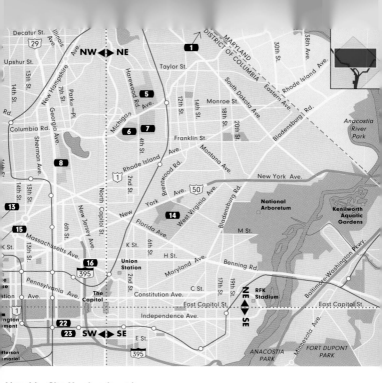

Listed by Site Number (cont.)

14 Gallaudet University

15 Strayer College

16 Georgetown Law Center

17 George Washington University

18 George Washington University School of Medicine

19 George Washington University School of Law

20 Marymount

21 George Mason School of Law

22 Department of Agriculture Graduate School

23 National Defense University

Listed Alphabetically (cont.)

Howard University, 8. 2400 6th St NW
☎ 806–6100

Johns Hopkins University, Nitze School of Advanced International Studies, 13. 1740 Massachusetts Ave NW ☎ 663–5700

Marymount University, 20.
2807 N. Glebe Rd Arlington, VA
☎ 703/522–5600

Mt Vernon College, 9.
2100 Foxhall Rd NW ☎ 242–6600

National Defense University Fort Lesley McNair, 23. 300 5th St SW
☎ 685–4700

St Paul's College, 7. 3015 4th St NE
☎ 832–6262

Strayer University, 15.
125 15th St NW ☎ 408–2400

Trinity College, 6.
125 Michigan Ave NE ☎ 884–9000

University of the District of Columbia, 2.
4200 Connecticut Ave NW
☎ 274–5000

University of Maryland, 1.
University Blvd, College Park, MD
☎ 301/405–1000

Wesley Theological Seminary, 3.
4500 Massachusetts Ave NW
☎ 885–8600

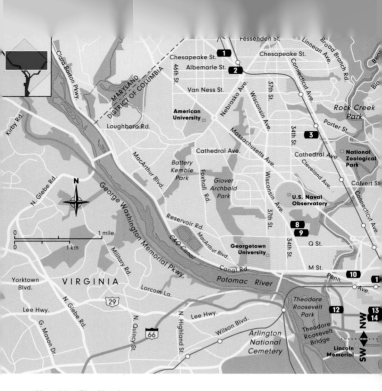

Listed by Site Number

1	National Library of Medicine	7	Woodridge	13	Daughters of the American Revolution
2	Tenley-Friendship	8	Georgetown	14	Organization of American States
3	Cleveland Park	9	Dumbarton Oaks	15	Martin Luther King Jr Memorial
4	Petworth	10	West End	16	American Art/Portrait Gallery
5	National Agricultural	11	Foundation Center		
6	Mt Pleasant	12	National Academy of Sciences		

Listed Alphabetically

Air & Space, 22. Independence Ave & 6th St SW ☎ 633–2320

American Art/Portrait Gallery, 16. 750 9th St NW ☎ 275–1912

American History, 18. Constitution Ave & 12th St SW ☎ 357–2414

Anacostia, 29. Good Hope Rd & 18th St SE ☎ 698–1190

Cleveland Park, 3. 3310 Connecticut Ave NW ☎ 282–3080

Daughters of the American Revolution, 13. 1776 D St NW ☎ 628–1776

Dumbarton Oaks, 9. 1703 32nd St NW ☎ 339–6401

Folger Shakespeare, 27. 201 E Capitol St SE ☎ 544–4600

Foundation Center, 11. 1627 K St NW ☎ 331–1400

Freer and Sackler Library, 20. 1050 Independence Ave SW ☎ 633–0477

Georgetown , 8. 3260 R St NW ☎ 282–0220

Library of Congress, 26. 101 Independence Ave SE ☎ 707–5000

Martin Luther King Jr Memorial, 15. 901 G St NW ☎ 727–1111

Mt Pleasant, 6. Lamont St & 16th St NW ☎ 671–0200

National Academy of Sciences, 12. 500 5th St NW ☎ 334–2125

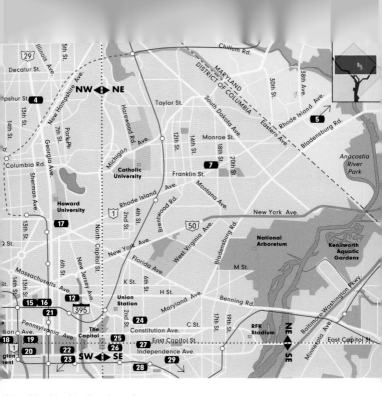

Listed by Site Number (cont.)

17 Watha T Daniel
18 American History
19 Natural History
20 Freer and Sackler Library
21 National Archives

22 Air & Space
23 Southwest
24 Northeast
25 Supreme Court
26 Library of Congress

27 Folger Shakespeare
28 Southeast
29 Anacostia

Listed Alphabetically

National Agricultural, 5.
10301 Baltimore Ave, Beltsville, MD
☎ 301/504-5755

National Archives, 21.
Pennsylvania Ave & 7th St NW
☎ 501-5402

National Library of Medicine, 1.
8600 Rockville Pk, Bethesda, MD
☎ 301/496-6308

Natural History, 19.
Constitution Ave & 10th St NW
☎ 357-1496

Northeast, 24. 330 7th St NE
☎ 698-3320

Organization of American States, 14.
Constitution Ave & 19th St NW
☎ 458-6037

Petworth, 4. 4200 Kansas Ave NW
☎ 541-6300

Southeast, 28. 403 7th St SE
☎ 698-3377

Southwest, 23. 900 Wesley Pl SW
☎ 724-4752

Supreme Court, 25. Maryland Ave
& 1st St NE ☎ 479-3175

Tenley-Friendship, 2. 4450
Wisconsin Ave NW ☎ 282-3090

Watha T Daniel, 17. 801 Rhode
Island Ave NW ☎ 671-0212

West End, 10. 1101 24th St NW
☎ 724-8707

Woodridge, 7. 1801 Hamlin St NE
☎ 541-6226

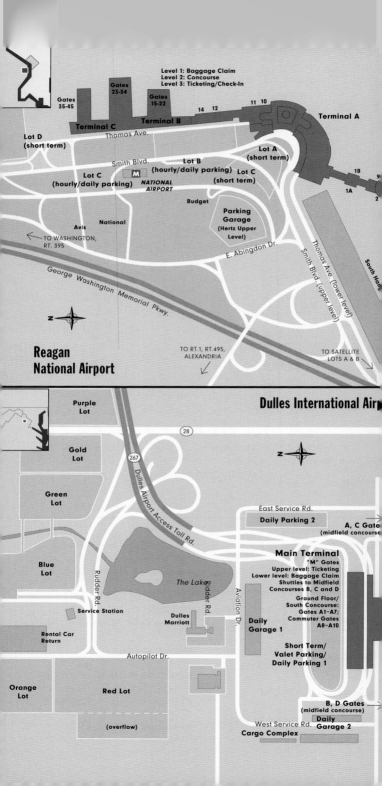

Reagan National Airport

Level 1: Baggage Claim
Level 2: Concourse
Level 3: Ticketing/Check-In

Gates 23–34

Gates 35–45

Gates 15–22

14   12   11   10

Terminal C   **Terminal B**   **Terminal A**

1B

9

1A   2

Lot D (short term)

Thomas Ave.

Lot A (short term)

Smith Blvd.

Lot B (hourly/daily parking)

Lot C (hourly/daily parking)

Lot C (short term)

M

NATIONAL AIRPORT

Budget

Parking Garage (Hertz Upper Level)

← TO WASHINGTON, RT. 395

Avis

National

E. Abingdon Dr.

Thomas Ave. (upper level)

Smith Blvd. (lower level)

South Ham[...]

George Washington Memorial Pkwy.

N

TO RT.1, RT.495, ALEXANDRIA

TO SATELLITE LOTS A & B

Dulles International Air[...]

Purple Lot

Gold Lot

(28)

267

Green Lot

East Service Rd.

Daily Parking 2

A, C Gate[...] (midfield concourse[...]

Blue Lot

Dulles Airport Access Toll Rd.

Rudder Rd.

The Lake

Rudder Rd.

Aviation Dr.

N

Main Terminal
"M" Gates
Upper level: Ticketing
Lower level: Baggage Claim
Shuttles to Midfield
Concourses B, C and D

Ground Floor/
South Concourse:
Gates A1–A7;
Commuter Gates
A8–A10

Service Station

Dulles Marriott

Daily Garage 1

**Short Term/
Valet Parking/
Daily Parking 1**

Rental Car Return

Autopilot Dr.

Orange Lot

Red Lot

(overflow)

B, D Gates (midfield concourse)

West Service Rd.

Daily Garage 2

Cargo Complex

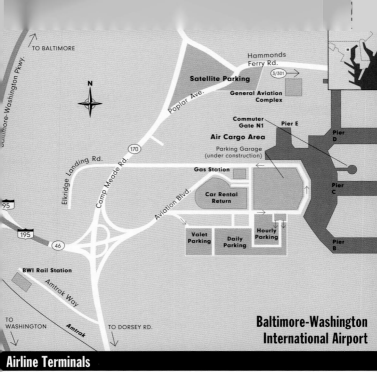

Baltimore-Washington International Airport

Airline Terminals

AIRLINES	REAGAN/NAT'L	DULLES	BWI
Aeroflot ☎ 800/340-6400		B	
Air Canada ☎ 888/247-2262	C	C	E
Air France ☎ 800/321-4538		B	
Air Jamaica ☎ 800/523-5585			E
Air Tran ☎ 800/247-8726		B	D
Alaska Airlines ☎ 800/252-7522	A	D	
All Nippon (ANA) ☎ 800/235-9262		B	
America West ☎ 800/235-9292	B	D	D
American ☎ 800/433-7300	B	D	C
Atlantic Coast ☎ 800/241-6522		A	
British Airways ☎ 800/247-9297		D	E
Continental ☎ 800/525-0280	B	B	D
Continental Express ☎ 800/525-0280	B	B	
Delta ☎ 800/221-1212	B	B	C
DeltaConnection ☎ 800/221-1212	B		
Ethiopian Air ☎ 800/445-2733		D	
Frontier Airlines ☎ 800/432-1359	B		D
Icelandair ☎ 800/223-5500			E
Jet Blue ☎ 800/538-2583		B	
KLM ☎ 800/225-2525		B	
Korean Air ☎ 800/438-5000		B	
Lufthansa ☎ 800/645-3880		C	
Midway ☎ 800/446-4392	A		
Midwest Express ☎ 800/452-2022	B		D
Northwest ☎ 800/225-2525	A	B	D
Saudi Arabian ☎ 800/472-8342		A	
Southwest ☎ 800/435-9792			B,C
Swiss Air ☎ 877/359-7947		D	
United ☎ 800/241-6522	C	C,D	D
United Express ☎ 800/241-6522		A	
US Airways ☎ 800/428-4322	B,C	B	D
US Airways Express ☎ 800/428-4322	C		
Virgin Atlantic ☎ 800/862-8621		B	

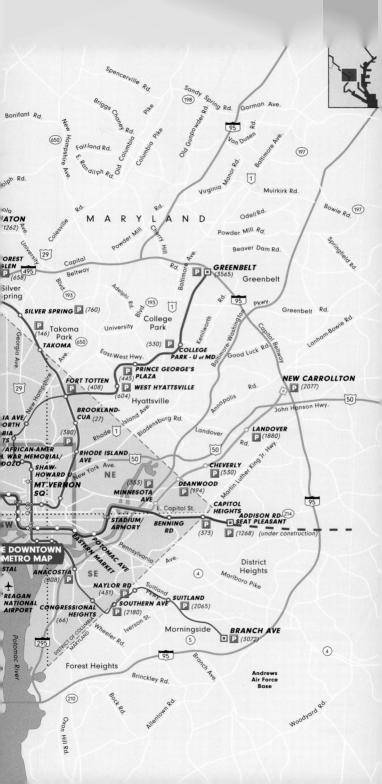

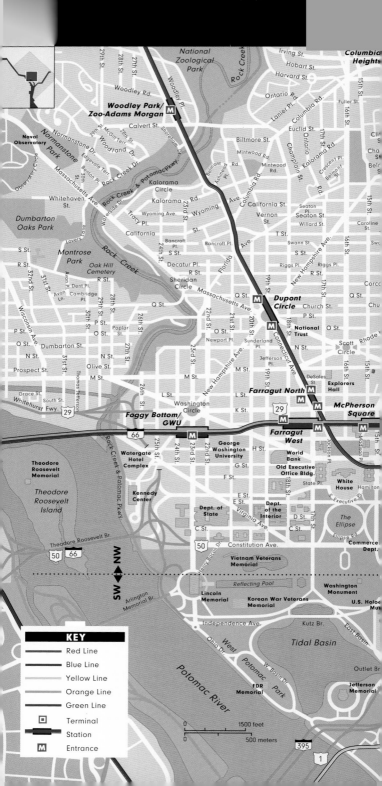

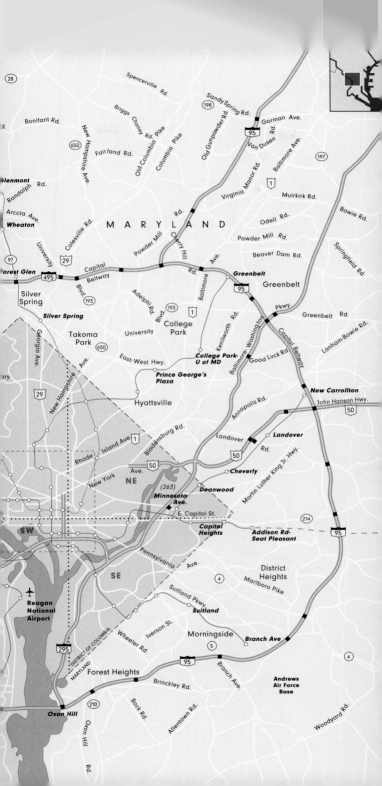

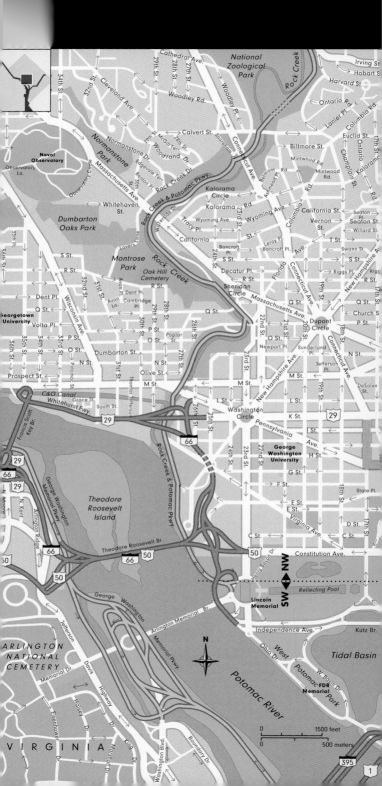

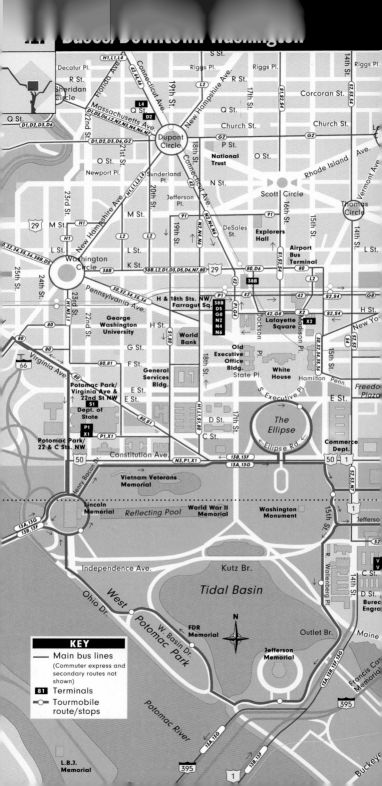

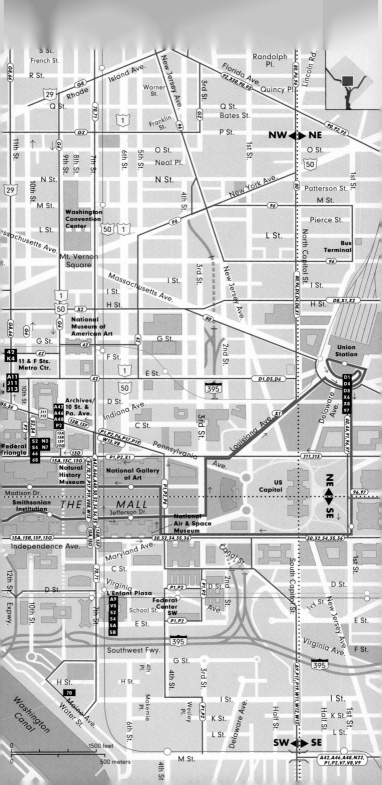

MAP 18 Buses/Arlington & National Airport

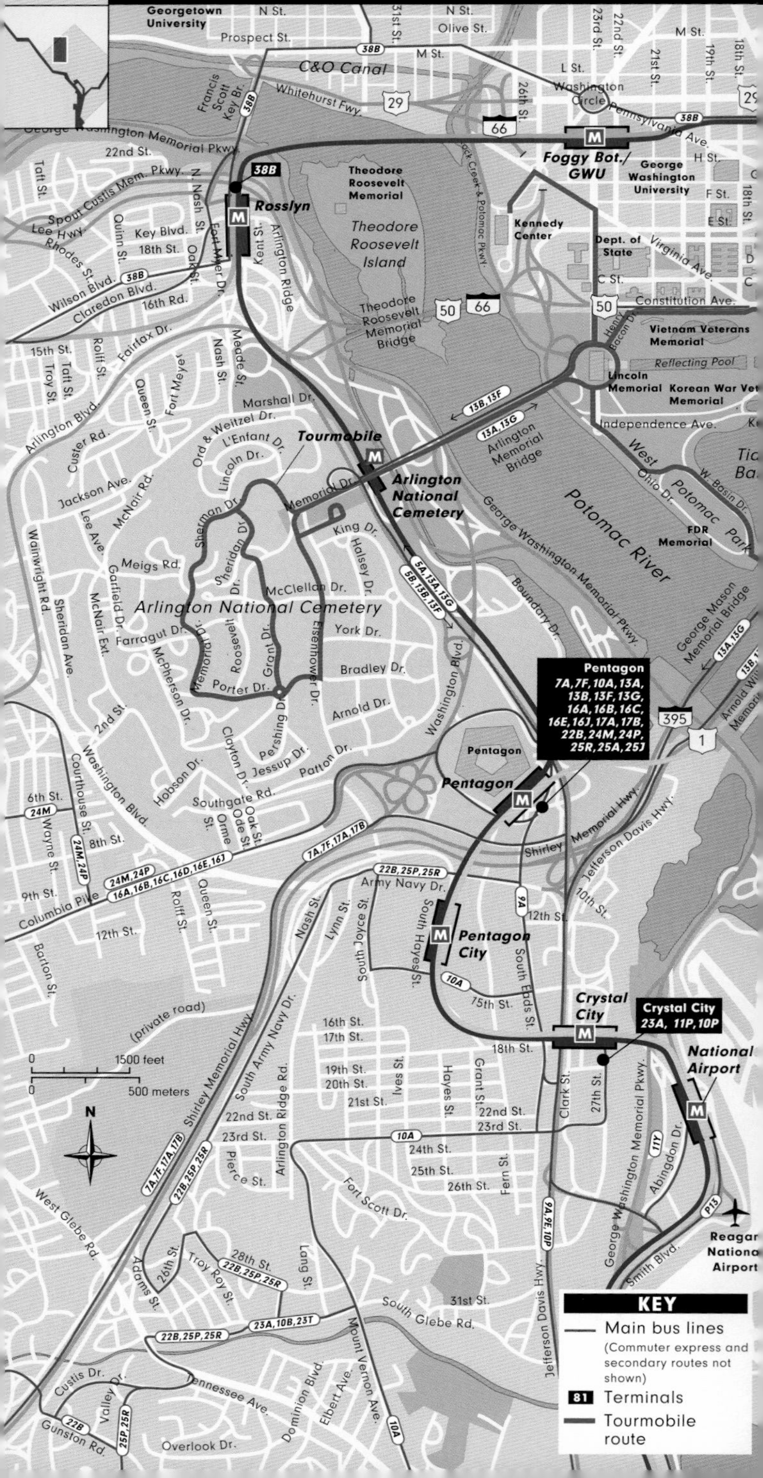

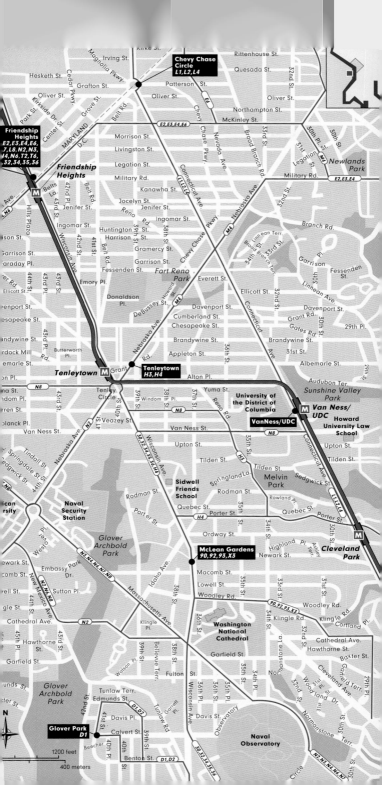

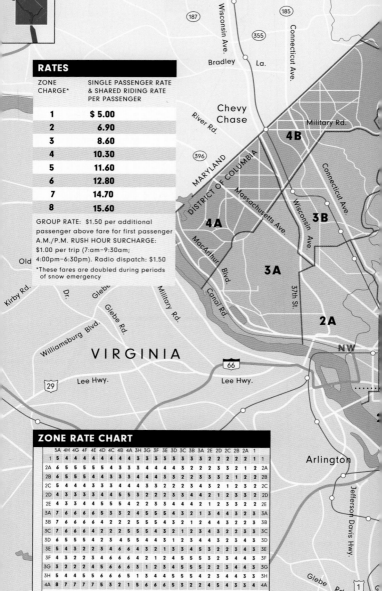

RATES

ZONE CHARGE*	SINGLE PASSENGER RATE & SHARED RIDING RATE PER PASSENGER
1	$ 5.00
2	6.90
3	8.60
4	10.30
5	11.60
6	12.80
7	14.70
8	15.60

GROUP RATE: $1.50 per additional passenger above fare for first passenger
A.M./P.M. RUSH HOUR SURCHARGE: $1.00 per trip (7:am–9:30am; 4:00pm–6:30pm). Radio dispatch: $1.50

*These fares are doubled during periods of snow emergency

ZONE RATE CHART

	5A	4H	4G	4F	4E	4D	4C	4B	4A	3H	3G	3F	3E	3D	3C	3B	3A	2E	2D	2C	2B	2A	1	
1	5	4	4	4	4	4	4	4	4	3	3	3	3	3	3	3	3	2	2	2	2	1	1	1
2A	6	5	5	5	5	4	3	3	4	3	3	4	3	3	3	3	2	2	2	3	3	1	2	2A
2B	6	5	5	5	4	4	3	3	4	4	4	3	3	2	2	3	3	2	1	2	1	2	2	2B
2C	5	4	4	4	3	3	3	3	4	4	3	2	2	2	3	3	2	1	2	3	2	2	2	2C
2D	4	3	3	4	4	3	4	4	5	5	3	2	2	3	4	4	2	1	2	3	3	3	2	2D
2E	4	3	3	4	4	5	4	4	5	4	2	2	3	3	4	4	2	1	2	3	3	3	2	2E
3A	7	6	6	6	5	3	3	4	5	5	5	4	3	2	1	4	4	3	2	3	3	4	3	3A
3B	7	6	6	6	4	2	2	2	5	5	4	3	2	1	2	4	4	2	2	2	3	3	3	3B
3C	7	6	6	6	4	2	2	5	5	5	4	3	2	1	2	3	4	3	2	2	2	3	3	3C
3D	6	5	5	5	4	2	3	4	5	5	4	3	1	2	3	4	4	3	2	3	3	4	3	3D
3E	5	4	3	2	2	3	4	6	6	6	4	1	2	3	4	5	5	3	2	2	3	4	3	3E
3F	4	3	2	2	3	4	6	6	6	7	1	2	4	5	5	5	3	2	2	3	3	4	3	3F
3G	3	2	2	3	4	5	6	6	7	1	2	3	4	5	6	6	3	3	3	4	4	5	4	3G
3H	5	4	4	5	6	6	6	5	1	3	4	4	5	5	4	2	4	3	2	3	4	4	5	3H
4A	8	7	7	7	5	3	2	1	6	6	6	5	3	2	2	4	5	3	3	4	4	5	4	4A
4B	8	7	7	6	4	2	1	2	6	6	6	5	4	3	3	4	5	3	3	4	4	5	4	4B
4C	8	7	6	5	2	1	3	6	6	6	4	3	2	2	3	3	5	3	3	4	4	4	4	4C
4D	7	6	6	5	4	1	2	4	5	6	5	4	3	2	3	4	5	3	3	4	4	4	4	4D
4E	4	4	5	2	1	4	6	6	7	5	4	2	2	4	4	6	6	3	3	4	5	4	4	4E
4F	5	3	2	1	2	5	6	7	7	5	2	2	2	5	6	6	3	3	4	5	5	6	5	4F
4G	2	2	1	2	3	6	7	7	7	4	2	3	3	6	6	6	3	3	4	5	5	6	5	4G
4H	2	1	2	3	4	6	7	7	7	4	3	4	5	6	6	7	4	4	5	6	6	6	5	4H
5A	1	2	3	4	5	6	8	8	8	5	3	4	5	6	7	7	4	4	5	6	6	6	5	5A
	5A	4H	4G	4F	4E	4D	4C	4B	4A	3H	3G	3F	3E	3D	3C	3B	3A	2E	2D	2C	2B	2A	1D	

To Subzone

From Subzone

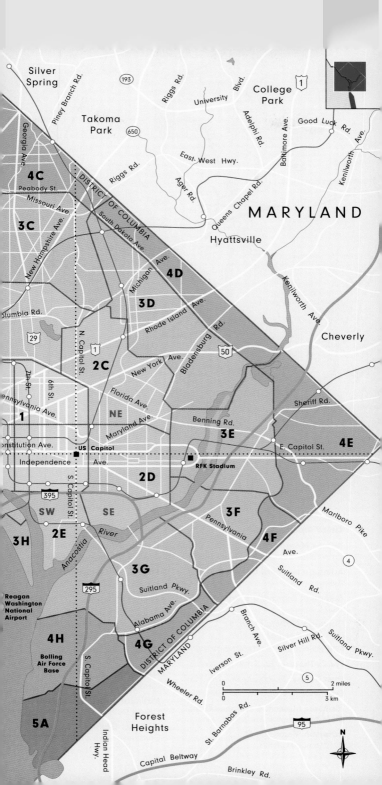

Listed Alphabetically

Adams Morgan, 3.
Columbia Rd & 18th St NW

Arlington National Cemetery, 14.
Arlington, VA

Bureau of Engraving & Printing, 27.
1400 C St SW

Corcoran Gallery of Art, 9.
New York Ave & 17th St NW

FDR Memorial, 13. 900 Ohio Dr SW

Ford's Theatre, 18. 511 10th St NW

Freer Gallery, 28. Jefferson Dr & 12th St SW

Georgetown, 5. Wisconsin Ave & M St NW

**Hirshhorn Museum & Sculpture Gdns,
31.** Independence Ave & 7th St SW

Jefferson Memorial, 35.
W Potomac Park SW

Kennedy Center, 6. New Hampshire
Ave & Rock Creek Pkwy NW

Korean War Veterans Memorial, 12.
French Dr SW

Lincoln Memorial, 11. Constitution
Ave & 23rd St SW

National Air & Space Museum, 32.
Independence Ave & 6th St SW

National Arboretum, 17.
3501 New York Ave NE

National Archives, 25.
Constitution Ave & 8th St NW

National Building Museum, 21.
F & 4th Sts NW

National Gallery of Art, 33.
Constitution Ave & 7th St NW

isted Alphabetically (cont.)

National Museum of African Art, 30. 50 Independence Ave SW

National Museum of American Art, 9. G & 8th Sts NW

National Museum of American History, 23. Constitution Ave & 14th St NW

National Museum of Natural History, 24. Constitution Ave & 10th St NW

National Museum of Women in the Arts, 15. 1250 New York Ave NW

National Portrait Gallery, 20. & 8th Sts NW

National Shrine of the Immaculate Conception, 16. Michigan Ave & 4th St NE

National Zoo, 2. 000 Connecticut Ave NW

Pentagon, 36. off I-395, Arlington, VA

Phillips Collection, 4. 1600 21st St NW

Renwick Gallery, 7. Pennsylvania Ave & 17th St NW

Smithsonian Castle, 29. 1000 Jefferson Dr SW

Union Station, 22. 50 Mass Ave

US Capitol, 34. 1st St NE

US Holocaust Memorial Museum, 26. 200 Raoul Wallenberg Pl SW

Vietnam Veterans Memorial, 10. Constitution Ave & 21st St NW

Washington National Cathedral, 1. Wisconsin & Massachusetts Aves NW

Waterfront, 37. Maine Ave SW

White House, 8. 1600 Pennsylvania Ave NW

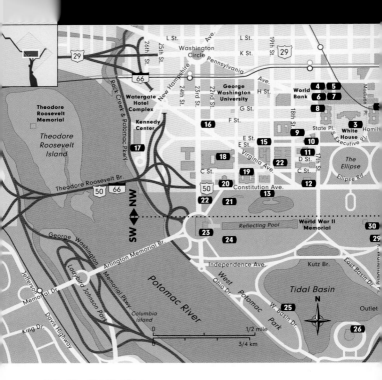

Listed by Site Number

1 National Museum of Women in the Arts
2 Treasury
3 White House
4 New Executive Office Building
5 Renwick Gallery
6 Decatur House
7 Blair House
8 Old Executive Office Building
9 Octagon House
10 Corcoran Gallery
11 DAR Museum
12 Organization of American States
13 Constitution Gardens
14 Dept of the Interior
15 Office of Personnel Management
16 Pan-American Health Organization
17 Kennedy Center
18 State Department
19 Federal Reserve
20 National Academy of Sciences

21 Vietnam Veterans Memorial
22 Vietnam Women's Memorial
23 Lincoln Memorial
24 Korean War Veterans Memorial
25 FDR Memorial
26 Jefferson Memorial
27 Bureau of Engraving & Printing
28 US Holocaust Memorial Museum
29 Sylvan Theater
30 Washington Monument
31 Department of Agriculture
32 Freer Gallery
33 Sackler Gallery
34 Enid Haupt Memorial Garden
35 Smithsonian Castle
36 National Museum of African Art
37 Arts and Industries Building
38 Sculpture Garden

39 Hirshhorn Museum
40 Federal Aviation Administration
41 Energy Department Forrestal Building
42 General Services Administration
43 Department of Housing & Urban Development
44 Department of Transportation
45 Education Department
46 National Air & Space Museum
47 National Museum of the American Indian
48 Voice of America
49 Department of Health & Human Services
50 US Botanic Garden
51 US Capitol
52 Rayburn House Office Building
53 Longworth House Office Building

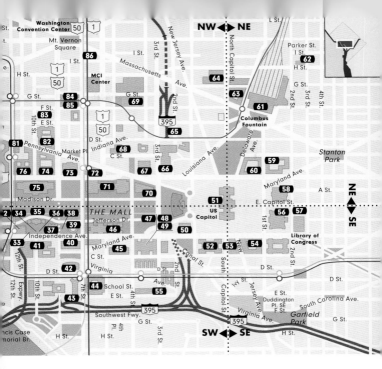

Listed by Site Number (cont.)

54 Cannon House Office Building

55 National Aeronautics & Space Administration

56 Library of Congress

57 Folger Shakespeare Library

58 Supreme Court

59 Dirksen Senate Office Building

59 Hart Senate Office Building

60 Russell Senate Office Building

61 Union Station

62 Capital Children's Museum

63 National Capitol Post Office / National Postal Museum

64 Government Printing Office

65 US Tax Court

66 Department of Labor

67 US Courthouse

68 DC Superior Court

69 National Building Museum

70 National Gallery of Art (east wing)

71 National Gallery of Art (west wing)

72 Federal Trade Commission

73 National Archives

74 Justice Department

75 National Museum of Natural History

76 Internal Revenue Service

77 National Museum of American History

78 Department of Commerce

78 National Aquarium

79 Executive Office of the Mayor

80 Customs Service

81 Old Post Office Pavilion

82 FBI

83 Ford's Theatre

84 National Portrait Gallery

85 National Museum of American Art

86 Alcohol, Tobacco & Firearms

Listed Alphabetically

Alcohol, Tobacco & Firearms, 86. 650 Massachusetts Ave NW ☎ 927-7777

Arts and Industries Bldg, 37. 900 Jefferson Dr SW ☎ 357-2700

Blair House, 4. 1651 Pennsylvania Ave NW ☎ 879-7880

Bureau of Engraving & Printing, 27. C St & 14th SW ☎ 874-3019

Cannon House Office Building, 54. Independence Ave & 1st St SE ☎ 224-3121

Capital Children's Museum, 62. 800 3rd St NE ☎ 675-4120

Constitution Gardens, 13. Between Washington Monument & Lincoln Memorial ☎ 426-6841

Corcoran Gallery, 10. 500 17th St NW ☎ 639-1700

Customs Service, 80. 1300 Pennsylvania Ave NW ☎ 354-1000

DAR Museum, 11. 1776 D St NW ☎ 879-3241

DC Superior Court, 68. 500 Indiana Ave NW ☎ 879-1010

Decatur House, 6. 1610 H St NW ☎ 842-0920

Department of Agriculture, 31. 1400 Independence Ave SW ☎ 720-2791

Department of Commerce, 78. Constitution Ave & 14th St NW ☎ 482-2000

Department of Education, 45. 400 Maryland Ave SW ☎ 401-2000

Dept of Energy/Forrestal Building, 41. 1000 Independence Ave SW ☎ 586-5000

Department of Health & Human Services, 49. 200 Independence Ave SW ☎ 619-0257

Department of Housing & Urban Development, 43. 451 7th St SW ☎ 708-1422

Department of the Interior, 14. 1849 C St NW ☎ 208-3100

Department of Labor, 66. 200 Constitution Ave NW ☎ 693-6660

Department of Transportation, 44. 400 7th St SW ☎ 366-4000

Dirksen Senate Office Building, 59. Constitution Ave & 1st St NE ☎ 224-3121

Enid Haupt Memorial Garden, 34. 1050 Independence Ave SW ☎ 357-2700

Executive Office of the Mayor, 79. 1350 Pennsylvania NW ☎ 727-2980

FBI, 82. 935 Pennsylvania Ave NW ☎ 324-3000

FDR Memorial, 25. W Basin Dr SW ☎ 426-6841

Federal Aviation Administration, 40. 800 Independence Ave SW ☎ 267-3484

Federal Reserve, 19. C St & 20th St NW ☎ 452-3000

Federal Trade Commission, 72. 600 Pennsylvania Ave NW ☎ 326-2222

Folger Shakespeare Library, 57. 201 E Capitol St SE ☎ 544-4600

Ford's Theatre, 83. 511 10th St NW ☎ 426-6924

Freer Gallery, 32. Jefferson Dr & 12th St SW ☎ 633-4880

General Services Administration, 42. D St & 7th St SW ☎ 708-5082

Government Printing Office, 64. 732 N Capitol St NW ☎ 512-0000

Hart Senate Office Building, 59. Constitution Ave & 2nd St NE ☎ 224-3121

Hirshhorn Museum, 39. Independence Ave & 7th St SW ☎ 357-2700

Internal Revenue Service, 76. 1111 Constitution Ave NW ☎ 622-5000

Jefferson Memorial, 26. 15th St SW at Tidal Basin ☎ 426-6841

Justice Department, 74. 950 Pennsylvania Ave NW ☎ 514-2000

Kennedy Center, 17. New Hampshire Ave & 25th St ☎ 467-4600

Korean War Veterans Memorial, 24. Indepedence Ave SW at Lincoln Memorial ☎ 426-6841

Library of Congress, 56. Independence Ave & First St NE ☎ 707-8000

Lincoln Memorial, 23. Constitution Ave and 23rd St SW ☎ 426-6841

Longworth House Office Building, 53. Independence Ave and New Jersey Ave SE ☎ 224-3121

National Academy of Sciences, 20. 2101 Constitution Ave NW ☎ 334-2000

Listed Alphabetically (cont.)

National Aeronautics & Space Administration, 55. 300 E St SW ☎ 358-0000

National Air & Space Museum, 46. Independence Ave & 6th St SW ☎ 357-2700

National Aquarium, 78. Constitution Ave & 14th St NW ☎ 482-2825

National Archives, 73. Constitution Ave & 7th St NW ☎ 501-5000

National Building Museum, 69. 401 F St NW ☎ 272-2448

National Capitol Post Office / National Postal Museum, 63. 2 Massachusetts Ave NE ☎ 357-2700

National Gallery of Art (east wing), 70. Constitution Ave & 4th St NW ☎ 737-4215

National Gallery of Art (west wing), 71. Constitution Ave & 6th St NW ☎ 737-4215

National Museum of African Art, 36. 950 Independence Ave SW ☎ 357-2700

National Museum of American Art, 85. G & 8th Sts NW ☎ 357-2700

National Museum of American History, 77. Constitution Ave & 14th St NW ☎ 357-2700

National Museum of the American Indian, 47. Independence Ave & Maryland Ave SE ☎ 357-1300

National Museum of Natural History, 75. Constitution Ave & 10th St NW ☎ 357-2700

National Museum of Women in the Arts, 1. 1250 New York Ave NW ☎ 783-5000

National Portrait Gallery, 84. G & 8th Sts NW ☎ 357-2700

New Executive Office Building, 4. 725 17th St NW ☎ 395-3000

Octagon House, 9. 1799 New York Ave NW ☎ 638-3105

Old Executive Office Building, 8. 625 17th St NW ☎ 395-3000

Old Post Office Pavilion, 81. 1100 Pennsylvania Ave NW ☎ 289-4224

Office of Personnel Management, 15. 1900 E St NW ☎ 606-1800

Organization of American States, 12. Constitution Ave & 17th St NW ☎ 458-3000

Pan-American Health Organization, 16. 525 23rd St NW ☎ 974-3000

Rayburn House Office Building, 52. Independence Ave & South Capitol St SW ☎ 224-3121

Renwick Gallery, 5. Pennsylvania Ave & 17th St NW ☎ 357-2700

Russell Senate Office Building, 60. Constitution Ave & Delaware Ave NE ☎ 224-3121

Sackler Gallery, 33. 1050 Independence Ave SW ☎ 633-4880

Sculpture Garden, 38. Independence Ave & 8th St NW ☎ 357-2700

Smithsonian Castle, 35. 1000 Jefferson Dr SW ☎ 357-2700

State Dept, 18. 2201 C St NW ☎ 647-4000

Supreme Court, 58. 1 First St NE ☎ 479-3000

Sylvan Theater, 29. Independence Ave & 15th St SW ☎ 426-6841

Treasury, 2. Pennsylvania Ave & 15th St NW ☎ 622-2000

Union Station, 61. 50 Massachusetts Ave NE ☎ 371-9441

US Botanic Garden, 50. 100 Maryland Ave SW ☎ 225-8333

US Capitol, 51. Capitol Hill ☎ 224-3121

US Courthouse, 67. 333 Constitution Ave NW ☎ 354-3000

US Holocaust Memorial Museum, 28. 100 Raoul Wallenberg Pl SW ☎ 488-0400

US Tax Court, 65. 400 2nd St NW ☎ 606-8754

Vietnam Veterans Memorial, 21. Constitution Ave & 21st St NW ☎ 426-6841

Vietnam Women's Memorial, 22. Constitution Gardens, Constitution Ave & 23rd St NW ☎ 426-6841

Voice of America, 48. 330 Independence Ave SW ☎ 619-4700

Washington Monument, 30. Constitution Ave & 15th St NW ☎ 426-6841

White House, 3. 1600 Pennsylvania Ave NW ☎ 456-7041

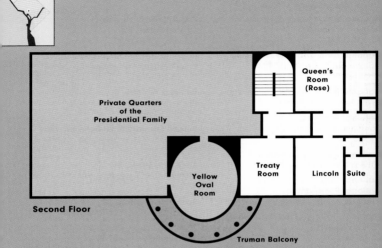

Second Floor

Private Quarters of the Presidential Family

Queen's Room (Rose)

Yellow Oval Room

Treaty Room

Lincoln Suite

Truman Balcony

Main Floor

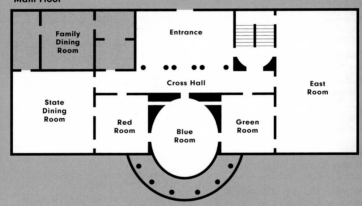

Family Dining Room

Entrance

State Dining Room

Cross Hall

East Room

Red Room

Blue Room

Green Room

Ground Floor

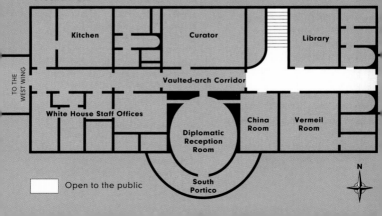

Kitchen

Curator

Library

TO THE WEST WING

Vaulted-arch Corridor

White House Staff Offices

Diplomatic Reception Room

China Room

Vermeil Room

South Portico

Open to the public

N

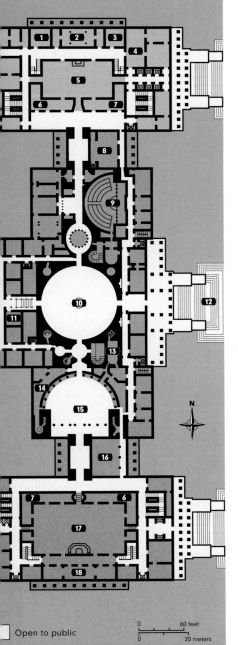

Listed by Site Number

1 President's Room
2 Marble Room (Senators' Retiring Room)
3 Ceremonial Office of the Vice President
4 Senators' Reception Room
5 Senate Chamber
6 Democratic Cloakrooms
7 Republican Cloakrooms
8 Senators' Conference Room
9 Old Senate Chamber
10 Rotunda
11 Prayer Room
12 East Front
13 Congresswomen's Suite
14 House Document Room
15 Statuary Hall
16 House Reception Room
17 House Chamber
18 Representatives' Retiring Rooms

N

0   60 feet
0   20 meters

Open to public

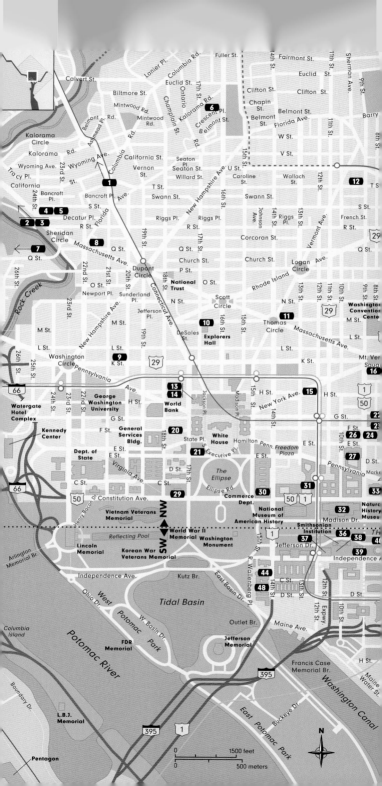

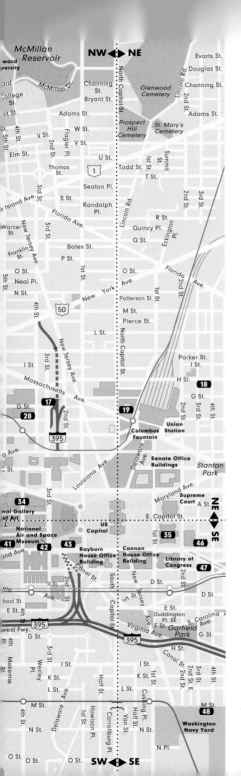

Listed Alphabetically

African Art (National Museum), 38. 950 Independence Ave SW ☎ 357-2700

Air & Space (National Museum), 41. Independence Ave & 6th St SW ☎ 357-2700

American Art (National Museum), 22. G & 8th Sts NW ☎ 357-2700

American History (National Museum), 31. Constitution Ave & 14th St NW ☎ 357-2700

American Indian (National Museum), 42. 4th St and Independence Ave SW ☎ 287-2020

Anacostia, 46. 1901 Fort Pl SE ☎ 357-2700

Art Museum of the Americas, 29. 201 18th St NW ☎ 458-6016

Arts and Industries, 39. 900 Jefferson Dr SW ☎ 357-2700

Bead Museum, 25. 400 7th St NW ☎ 624-4500

Black Fashion Museum, 12. 2007 Vermont Ave NW ☎ 667-0744

B'nai B'rith Klutznick National Jewish Museum, 9. 2020 K St NW ☎ 857-6583

Bureau of Engraving & Printing, 45. 1400 C St SW ☎ 874-3019

Capital Children's Museum, 18. 800 3rd St NE ☎ 675-4121

City Museum, 16. 801 K St NW ☎ 785-2068

Corcoran Gallery, 21. New York Ave & 17th St NW ☎ 639-1700

Decatur House, 14. 748 Jackson Pl NW ☎ 842-0920

Dumbarton Oaks, 7. 1703 32nd St NW ☎ 339-6401

FBI, 27. 935 Pennsylvania Ave NW ☎ 324-3000

Ford's Theatre & Lincoln Museum, 26. 511 10th St NW ☎ 426-6924

Frederick Douglass Nat'l Historic Site, 47. 1411 W St SE ☎ 426-5961

Hillwood Museum & Gardens, 2. 4155 Linnean Ave NW ☎ 686-5807

Hirshhorn, 40. Independence Ave & 7th St SW ☎ 357-2700

International Spy Museum, 24. 800 F St NW ☎ 393-7798

Jewish Historical Society, 17. 701 3rd St NW ☎ 789-0900

Library of Congress, 35. 10 First St SE ☎ 707-8000

Mary McLeod Bethune House, 11. 1318 Vermont Ave NW ☎ 673-2402

Meridian International Center, 6. 1624 Crescent Pl NW ☎ 667-6670

Nat'l Aquarium, 32. Constitution Ave & 14th St NW ☎ 482-2825

Nat'l Archives, 33. 800 Constitution Ave NW ☎ 501-5000

National Building Museum, 28. 401 F St NW ☎ 272-2448

Nat'l Gallery of Art, 34. Constitution Ave & 6th St NW ☎ 737-4215

National Geographic/Explorer's Hall, 10. M & 17th Sts NW ☎ 857-7588

National Portrait Gallery, 23. F & 8th Sts NW ☎ 357-2700

National Postal Museum, 19. 2 Massachusetts Ave NE ☎ 523-2022

Natural History (National Museum), 32. Constitution Ave & 10th St NW ☎ 357-2700

Naval Observatory, 3. Massachusetts Ave & 34th St NW ☎ 762-1467

Navy Museum, 48. Navy Yard, 901 M St SE ☎ 433-4882

Octagon House, 20. 1799 New York Ave NW ☎ 638-3105

Phillips Collection, 8. 1600 21st St NW ☎ 387-2151

Renwick Gallery, 13. Pennsylvania Ave & 17th St NW ☎ 357-2700

Sackler Gallery, 37. 1050 Independence Ave SW ☎ 357-4880

Smithsonian Institution (Castle), 36. 1000 Jefferson Dr NW ☎ 357-2700

Textile, 4. 2320 S St NW ☎ 667-0441

US Botanic Gardens, 43. Maryland Ave & 1st St SW ☎ 225-8333

US Holocaust Memorial Museum, 44. 200 Raoul Wallenberg Pl SW ☎ 488-0400

Washington Dolls' House & Toy Museum, 2. 5236 44th St NW ☎ 244-0024

Women in Arts (National Museum), 15. 1250 New York Ave NW ☎ 783-5000

Woodrow Wilson House, 5. 2340 S St NW ☎ 387-4062

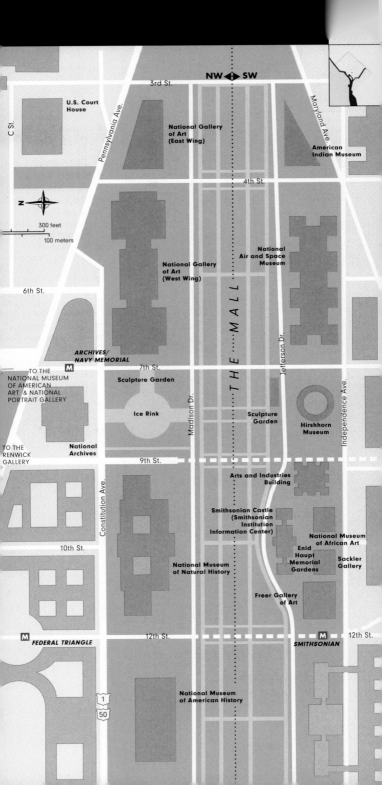

NW ◆ SW

3rd St.

U.S. Court House

National Gallery of Art (East Wing)

Maryland Ave.

Pennsylvania Ave.

American Indian Museum

C St.

4th St.

N

300 feet
100 meters

National Gallery of Art (West Wing)

National Air and Space Museum

6th St.

T H E   M A L L

Jefferson Dr.

ARCHIVES/ NAVY MEMORIAL

M

7th St.

Sculpture Garden

TO THE NATIONAL MUSEUM OF AMERICAN ART & NATIONAL PORTRAIT GALLERY

Ice Rink

Madison Dr.

Sculpture Garden

Hirshhorn Museum

Independence Ave.

TO THE RENWICK GALLERY

National Archives

9th St.

Arts and Industries Building

Smithsonian Castle (Smithsonian Institution Information Center)

National Museum of African Art

10th St.

Constitution Ave.

Enid Haupt Memorial Gardens

Sackler Gallery

National Museum of Natural History

Freer Gallery of Art

M

FEDERAL TRIANGLE

12th St.

M

SMITHSONIAN

12th St.

1
50

National Museum of American History

MAP 27 **National Gallery of Art/West Wing**

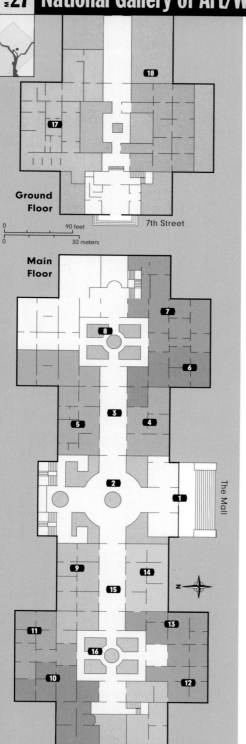

Ground Floor

7th Street

0 — 90 feet
0 — 30 meters

Main Floor

The Mall

Listed by Site Number

1 Mall Entrance
2 Rotunda
3 East Sculpture Hall
4 French Painting (17th & 18th Century)
5 French Painting (19th Century)
6 British Painting
7 American Painting
8 East Garden Court
9 Renaissance Painting (Florence & Central Italy)
10 Renaissance Painting (Venice & Northern Italy)
11 Italian Furniture & Sculpture
12 Italian Painting (17th & 18th Century)
13 Spanish Painting
14 Flemish & German Painting
15 West Sculpture Hall
16 European Sculpture (West Garden Court)
17 Sculpture & Decorative Arts
18 Lecture Hall

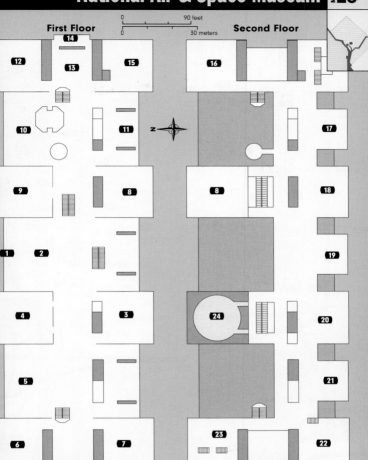

First Floor

Second Floor

0   90 feet
0   30 meters

N

Listed by Site Number

1   Main Entrance
2   Milestones of Flight
3   Early Flight
4   Museum Shop
5   Air Transportation
6   Flight Simulators
7   Golden Age of Flight
8   How Things Fly
9   Lockheed Martin
    IMAX Theater
10 Space Race
11 Looking at Earth
12 Space Flight &
    Rockets
13 Lunar Rovers

14 Wright Place
    Restaurant
15 Universe
16 Beyond the Limits
17 Apollo To The Moon
18 The Wright Brothers
19 Pioneers of Flight
20 Exploring the Planets
21 World War I Aviation
22 World War II
    Aviation
23 Sea-Air Operations
24 Albert Einstein
    Planetarium

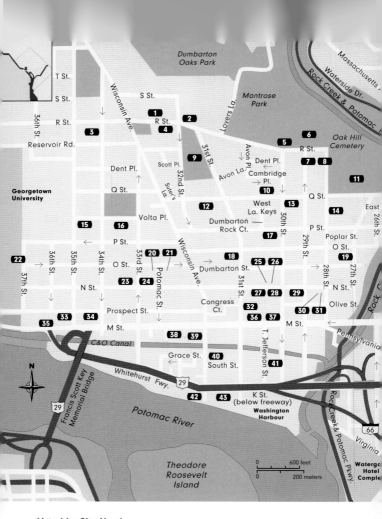

Listed by Site Number

1 Dougall House
2 Dumbarton Oaks
3 Mackall-Worthington House
4 Scott-Grant House
5 Oak Hill Cemetery Gatehouse
6 Oak Hill Cemetery
7 Mackall Square
8 Evermay
9 Tudor Place
10 Cooke's Row
11 Dumbarton House
12 Bowie-Sevier House
13 Francis Dodge House
14 Miller House

15 Alexander Melville Bell House
16 Pomander Walk
17 Linthicum House
18 Christ Church
19 Trentman House
20 Bodisco House
21 St John's Church
22 Georgetown Univ
23 Cox's Row
24 Smith Row
25 Loughboro-Paterson House
26 Wheatley House
27 Riggs-Riley House
28 Laird-Dunlop House

29 Foxall House
30 Decatur House
31 Gannt-Williams House
32 Custom House
33 Prospect House
34 Halcyon House
35 Exorcist Steps
36 Old Stone House
37 Thomas Sim Lee Corner
38 Georgetown Park
39 Vigilant Firehouse
40 Grace Epis. Church
41 C & O Canal (Barge)
42 Washington Harbour
43 Dodge Warehouse

Listed Alphabetically

Alexander Melville Bell House, 15.
152 35th St NW

Bodisco House, 20. 3322 O St NW

Bowie-Sevier House, 12. 3124 Q St NW

C & O Canal (Barge), 41.
1055 Thomas Jefferson St NW

Christ Church, 18.
O & 31st Sts NW

Cooke's Row, 10.
3007-29 Q St NW

Cox's Row, 23.
3327-39 N St NW

Custom House, 32.
1221 31st St NW

Decatur House, 30.
2812 N St NW

Dodge Warehouse, 43.
Wisconsin Ave & K St NW

Dougall House, 1.
3259 R St NW

Dumbarton House, 11.
2715 Q St NW

Dumbarton Oaks, 2.
1703 32nd St NW

Evermay, 8.
1628 28th St NW

Exorcist Steps, 35.
M & 36th Sts NW

Foxall House, 29.
2908 N St NW

Francis Dodge House, 13.
1517-37 30th St NW

Gannt-Williams House, 31.
2806 N St NW

Georgetown Park, 38.
3222 M St NW

Georgetown University, 22.
O & 37th Sts NW

Grace Episcopal Church, 40.
1041 Wisc Ave NW

Halcyon House, 34.
3400 Prospect St NW

Laird-Dunlop House, 28.
3014 N St NW

Linthicum House, 17.
3019 P St NW

Loughboro-Paterson House, 25.
3039-41 N St NW

Mackall Square, 7.
1633 29th St NW

Mackall-Worthington House, 3.
1686 34th St NW

Miller House, 14.
1524 28th St NW

Oak Hill Cemetery Gatehouse, 5.
R & 30th Sts NW

Oak Hill Cemetery, 6.
R & 30th Sts NW

Old Stone House, 36.
3051 M St NW

Pomander Walk, 16.
Volta Pl NW

Prospect House, 33.
3508 Prospect St NW

Riggs-Riley House, 27.
3038 N St NW

Scott-Grant House, 4.
3238 R St NW

Smith Row, 24.
3255-63 N St NW

St John's Church, 21.
3240 O St NW

Thomas Sim Lee Corner, 37.
3001-9 M St NW

Trentman House, 19.
1350 27th St NW

Tudor Place, 9.
1644 31st St NW

Vigilant Firehouse, 39.
1066 Wisconsin Ave NW

Washington Harbour, 42.
3020 K St NW

Wheatley House, 26.
3041-3 N St NW

MAP 30 Churches, Temples & Mosques

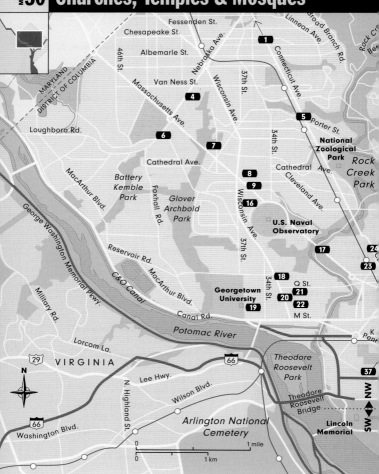

Listed by Site Number

1 Church of Jesus Christ of Latter-Day Saints
2 St Paul's (Rock Creek)
3 Franciscan Monastery
4 National Presbyterian
5 Adas Israel Synagogue
6 Metropolitan Memorial United Methodist
7 Washington Hebrew Congregation
8 Washington National Cathedral

9 Cathedral of St Sophia
10 St Stephen and the Incarnation
11 Sacred Heart
12 National Shrine of the Immaculate Conception
13 National Baptist Memorial
14 All Souls Unitarian
15 First Church of Christ, Scientist
16 Temple Micah
17 Islamic Center Mosque
18 Georgetown Lutheran

19 Holy Trinity
20 St John's (Georgetown)
21 Kesher Israel Synagogue
22 Mt Zion United Methodist
23 Friends Meeting of Washington
24 St Margaret's
25 St Augustine
26 Metropolitan Baptist
27 Foundry United Methodist
28 First Baptist
29 Grace Reformed

Listed by Site Number (cont.)

50 St Matthew's Cathedral

51 Metropolitan African Methodist Episcopal

52 National City Christian

53 Luther Place Memorial

54 Shiloh Baptist

55 Metropolitan Community Church

56 Mt Vernon Place United Methodist

57 Western Presbyterian

58 Third Christ, Scientist

59 St John's (Lafayette Sq)

40 Church of the Epiphany

41 Asbury United Methodist

42 St Patrick's

43 First Congregational

44 Calvary Baptist

45 St Mary's

46 New York Ave Presbyterian

47 Capitol Hill Presbyterian

48 Ebenezer United Methodist

49 Christ Church (Capitol Hill)

Churches, Temples & Mosques

Listed Alphabetically

Adas Israel Synagogue, 5.
2850 Quebec St NW
☎ 362–4433. Conservative

All Souls Unitarian, 14.
2835 16th St NW ☎ 332–5266

Asbury United Methodist, 41.
926 11th St NW ☎ 628–0009

Calvary Baptist, 44.
755 8th St NW ☎ 347–8355

Capitol Hill Presbyterian, 47
201 4th St SE ☎ 547–8676

Cathedral of St Sophia, 9.
Mass Ave & 36th St NW ☎ 333–4730.
Greek Orthodox

Christ Church (Capitol Hill), 49.
620 G St SE ☎ 547–9300. Episcopal

Church of Jesus Christ of Latter-Day Saints, 1. 10000 Stonybrook Dr Kensington, MD ☎ 301/588–6112 Mormon

Church of the Epiphany, 40.
1317 G St NW ☎ 347–2635. Episcopal

Ebenezer United Methodist, 48.
400 D St SE ☎ 544–1415

First Baptist, 28. 1328 16th St NW
☎ 387–2206

First Church of Christ, Scientist, 15.
1770 Euclid St NW ☎ 265–1390

First Congregational, 43. 945 G St NW
☎ 628–4317. United Church of Christ

Foundry United Methodist, 27.
1500 16th St NW ☎ 332–4010

Franciscan Monastery, 3. 1400 Quincy
St NE ☎ 526–6800. Roman Catholic

Friends Meeting of Washington, 23.
2111 Florida Ave NW ☎ 483–3310. Quaker

Georgetown Lutheran, 18.
1556 Wisconsin Ave NW ☎ 337–9070

Grace Reformed, 29. 1405 15th St NW
☎ 387–3131. United Church of Christ

Holy Trinity, 19. 3513 N St NW
☎ 337–2840. Roman Catholic

Islamic Center Mosque, 17. 2551
Massachusetts Ave NW ☎ 332–8343

Kesher Israel, 21. 2801 N St NW
☎ 333–4808. Orthodox

Luther Place Memorial, 33. 1226
Vermont Ave NW ☎ 667–1377. Lutheran

Metropolitan African Methodist Episcopal, 31. 1518 M St NW ☎ 331–1426

Metropolitan Baptist, 26.
1225 R St NW ☎ 238–5000

Metropolitan Community, 35.
474 Ridge St NW ☎ 638–7373

Metro Memorial United Methodist, 6
3401 Nebraska Ave NW ☎ 363–4900

Mt Vernon Place United Methodist, 36. 900 Massachusetts
Ave NW ☎ 347–9620

Mt Zion United Methodist, 22.
1334 29th St NW ☎ 234–0148

National Baptist Memorial, 13.
1501 Columbia Rd NW ☎ 265–1410

National City Christian, 32. 5 Thomas
Circle NW ☎ 232–0323. Disciples of Christ

National Presbyterian, 4.
4101 Nebraska Ave NW ☎ 537–0800

National Shrine of the Immaculate Conception, 12. 400 Michigan Ave
NE ☎ 526–8300. Roman Catholic

New York Ave Presbyterian, 46.
1313 New York Ave NW ☎ 393–3700

Sacred Heart, 11. Park Rd. & 16th St
NW ☎ 234–8000 Roman Catholic

Shiloh Baptist, 34. 1500 9th St NW
☎ 232–4200

St Augustine, 25. 1419 V St NW
☎ 265–1470. Roman Catholic

St John's (Georgetown), 20.
3240 O St NW ☎ 338–1796. Episcopal

St John's (Lafayette Sq), 39.
1525 H St NW ☎ 347–8766 Episcopal

St Margaret's, 24. 1830 Connecticut
Ave NW ☎ 232–2995 Episcopal

St Mary's, 45. 727 5th St NW
☎ 289–7770 Roman Catholic

St Matthew's Cathedral, 30.
1725 Rhode Is Ave NW ☎ 347–3215.
Roman Catholic

St Patrick's, 42. 619 10th St NW
☎ 347–2713. Roman Catholic

St Paul's (Rock Creek), 2.
Rock Creek Church Rd & Webster St NW
☎ 726–2080. Episcopal

St Stephen and the Incarnation, 10.
1525 Newton St NW ☎ 232–0900.
Episcopal

Temple Micah, 16. 2829 Wisconsin
Ave NW ☎ 342–9175. Reform

Third Church of Christ, Scientist, 38.
900 16th St NW ☎ 833–3325

Wash Hebrew Congregation, 7. 3935
Macomb St NW ☎ 362–7100. Reform

Washington National Cathedral, 8.
Wisconsin & Mass Aves NW
☎ 537–6200. Episcopal

Western Presbyterian, 37.
2401 Virginia Ave NW ☎ 835–8383

Listed Alphabetically

Abrams, Gen Creighton, 28

Barrow, T Sgt Joe Louis, 20

Bonesteel, Gen Chas III, 29

Boyington, Col "Pappy", 19

Bradley, Gen Omar, 1

Brown, Gen George S, 25

Bryan, Col William Jennings, 37

Byrd, R Adm Richard E, 17

Chaffee, Lt Comdr Roger, 31

Chennault, Lt Gen Claire Lee, 15

Decker, Gen George H, 23

Douglas, Justice William O, 7

Evers, Medgar, 3

Grissom, Lt Col Virgil I, 31

Halsey, Adm William Jr, 16

Henson, Matthew, 36

Holmes, Capt Oliver Wendell, 6

James, Gen Daniel, 13

Kennedy, Pres John F, 9

Kennedy, Robert F, 11

Kennedy Onassis, Jacqueline, 10

L'Enfant, Pierre Charles, 18

Leahy, Adm William D, 14

Lincoln, Capt Robt Todd, 4

Marshall, Gen George C, 22

Murphy, Audie, 28

Peary, R Adm Robert E, 35

Pershing, Gen George, 33

Reed, Maj Walter, 32

Rickover, Adm Hyman, 8

Scobee, Comdr Francis, 24

Sheridan, Gen Philip H, 12

Smith, Capt Michael, 21

Taft, Pres William H, 2

Wainwright, Gen Jonathan, 5

Warren, Chief Justice Earl, 26

Listed by Site Number

1	Eurythmy	**7**	Pebble Garden Fountain
2	Orbit	**8**	Francis Scott Key Memorial
3	Bairstow Eagle Lampposts	**9**	William O Douglas
4	Perry Lions	**10**	Buffaloes & Indian Heads
5	Kahlil Gibran	**11**	Gen Philip Sheridan
6	Sir Winston Churchill	**12**	Habitat

13	Maj Gen George B McClellan
14	Cubi XI
15	Mahatma Gandhi
16	Tomás Garrigue Masaryk
17	Taras Shevchenko

Listed by Site Number (cont.)

18 Rear Adm Samuel Francis Dupont Memorial Fountain

19 Cardinal James Gibbons

20 Guglielmo Marconi Memorial

21 Francis Asbury

22 Serenity

23 Dante

24 Joan of Arc

25 Pres James Buchanan

26 African-American Civil War Memorial

27 Maj Gen John A Logan

28 Samuel Gompers Memorial

29 Edmund Burke

30 Maj Gen George Thomas

31 Martin Luther

32 Dr Samuel Hahnemann

33 Lt Gen Winfield Brevet Scott

34 Australian Seal

Listed by Site Number (cont.)

35 Daniel Webster

36 Nuns of the Battlefield

37 Henry Wadsworth Longfellow

38 Lt Gen George Washington

39 Benito Juarez

40 Pres Theodore Roosevelt

41 America & War or Peace

42 Ascension

43 Expanding Universe Fountain

44 Albert Einstein

45 Vietnam Women's Memorial

46 Vietnam Veterans Memorial

47 Lincoln Memorial

48 Arts of Peace

49 Arts of War

50 Korean War Veterans Memorial

51 John Ericsson

52 FDR Memorial

53 Japanese Pagoda

54 Jefferson Memorial

55 The Awakening

56 Japanese Lantern

57 Commodore John Paul Jones Memorial

58 Gen José Gervasio Artigas

59 Gen Simon Bolivar

60 Queen Isabella I

61 South America

62 North America

63 Aztec Fountain

64 The Prophet Daniel

65 José Cecilio del Valle

66 Cordell Hull

67 Xochipilli, Aztec God of Flowers

68 Bullfinch Gatehouses

69 Second Division Monument

70 DAR Founders

71 Maj Gen John Rawlins

72 Abe Lincoln, Rail Joiner

73 Canova Lions

74 Red Cross Men & Women Killed in Service

75 Jane A Delano & the Nurses Who Died in Service in World War I

76 First Division Monument

77 Butt-Millet Memorial

78 Members of the American Institute of Architecture

79 Brig Gen Thaddeus Kosciuszko

80 Maj Gen Marquis Gilbert de Lafayette

81 Maj Gen Andrew Jackson

82 Maj Gen Baron von Steuben

83 Maj Gen Comte Jean de Rochambeau

84 Adm David Farragut

85 Brig Gen James B McPherson

86 Commodore John Barry

87 Albert Gallatin

88 Alexander Hamilton

89 Brig Gen Count Casimir Pulaski

90 Gen William Tecumseh Sherman

91 Settlers of the District of Columbia

92 Boy Scout Memorial

93 Bullfinch Gatehouses

94 Joseph Henry

95 Andrew Jackson Downing (Urn)

96 The Burghers of Calais

97 Infinity

98 Capt Nathan Hale

99 Benjamin Franklin

100 Acroterion Eagles

101 Andrew Mellon Memorial Fountain

102 Man Controlling Trade

103 Maj Gen Winfield Scott Hancock

104 Temperance Fountain

105 National Law Enforcement Memorial

106 Pegasus & Bellerophon

107 Sir William Blackstone

108 Chessmen

109 Justice John Marshall

110 Brig Gen Albert Pike

111 Acacia Griffins

112 Pres Robert A Taft Memorial

113 Peace Monument

114 Gen Ulysses S Grant Memorial

115 Pres James Garfield

116 Bartholdi Fountain

117 The Majesty of Law & The Spirit of Justice

118 Greek Vases

119 The Court of Neptune Fountain

120 Ethnological Heads

121 Equal Justice Under Law

122 Maj Gen Nathanael Greene

123 Shakespeare Scenes

124 Puck Fountain

125 Olive Risley Seward

126 Emancipation Monument

127 Mary McLeod Bethune

128 Christopher Columbus Memorial Fountain

129 Thomas Hopkins Gallaudet

130 Edward Miner Gallaudet

131 Christ, the Light of the World

132 St Jerome the Priest

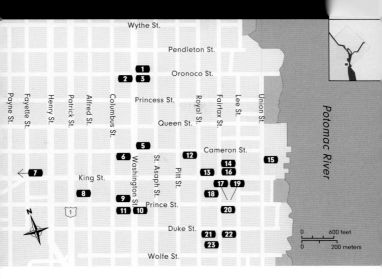

Listed by Site Number

1 Robert E Lee House

2 Edmund Jennings Lee House

3 Fendall-John L Lewis House

4 Lloyd House

5 Yeaton-Fairfax House

6 Christ Church

7 George Washington Masonic Nat'l Mem

8 Friendship Fire Co

9 William Fowle House

10 Confederate Statue "Appomattox"

11 Lyceum

12 Gadsby's Tavern Museum

13 Alexandria City Hall and Market Square

14 Bank of Alexandria

14 Carlyle House

15 Alexandria Archaeology Museum

15 Torpedo Factory Arts Center

16 Ramsay House

17 Thompson-Marshburn House

18 Stabler-Leadbeater Apothecary Shop

19 Athenaeum

20 Dr Wm Brown House

21 St Mary's Church

22 Dr James Craik House

23 Old Presbyterian Meeting House

Listed Alphabetically

Alexandria Archaeology Museum, 15. 105 N Union St

Alexandria City Hall and Market Square, 13. 301 King St

Athenaeum, 19. 201 Prince St

Bank of Alexandria, 14. 133 N Fairfax St

Carlyle House, 14. 123 N Fairfax St

Christ Church, 6. 118 N Washington St

Confederate Statue "Appomattox," 10. Prince St & S Washington St

Dr James Craik House, 22. 210 Duke St

Dr William Brown House, 20. 212 S Fairfax St

Edmund Jennings Lee House, 2. Oronoco & N Washington Sts

Fendall-Lewis House, 3. 614 Oronoco St

Friendship Fire Museum, 8. 107 S Alfred St

Gadsby's Tavern Museum, 12. 134-138 N Royal St

George Washington Masonic National Memorial, 7. 101 Callahan Dr

Lloyd House, 4. 220 N Washington St

Lyceum, 11. 201 S Washington St

Old Presbyterian Meeting House, 23. 321 S Fairfax St

Ramsay House (Visitor's Center), 16. King & N Fairfax Sts

Robert E Lee House, 1. 607 Oronoco St

St Mary's Church, 21. 310 Duke St

Stabler-Leadbeater Apothecary Shop, 18. 105-107 S Fairfax St

Thompson-Marshburn House, 17. 211 N Fairfax St

Torpedo Factory Arts Center, 15. 105 N Union St

Yeaton-Fairfax House, 5. 607 Cameron St

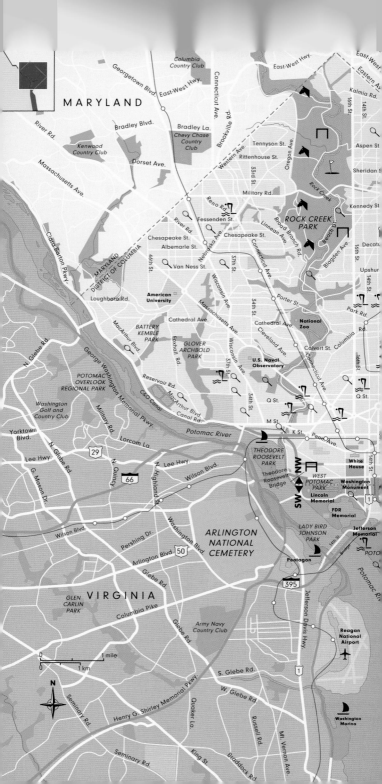

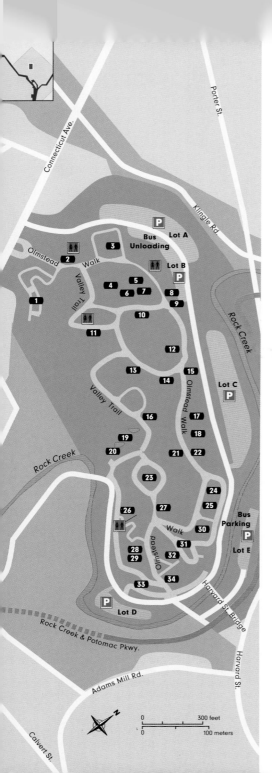

Listed by Site Number

1 Great Flight Exhibit
2 Visitors Center and Gift Shop
3 Cheetahs & Zebras
4 Kangaroos
5 Bison
6 Prairie Dogs
7 Pandas & Panda Cafe
8 Food & Gift Shops
9 Information & Strollers
10 Elephants & Giraffes
11 Bird House
12 Hippos & Rhinos
13 Golden Lion Tamarins
14 Beavers & Otters
15 Concession Stand
16 Mexican Wolves
17 Camels
18 Small Mammal House
19 Seals & Sea Lions
20 Spectacled Bears
21 Gibbon Ridge
22 Great Ape House
23 Bears
24 Reptile Center
25 Invertebrates
26 Amazonia
27 Lemur Island
28 Police & First Aid
29 Mane Restaurant
30 Monkey House
31 Lion-Tiger Hill
32 Bat Cave
33 Kid's Farm Construction
34 Information & Strollers

KEY

▬▬ Horse and Foot Trail
▬▬ Foot Trail
▬▬ Bike and Foot Trail

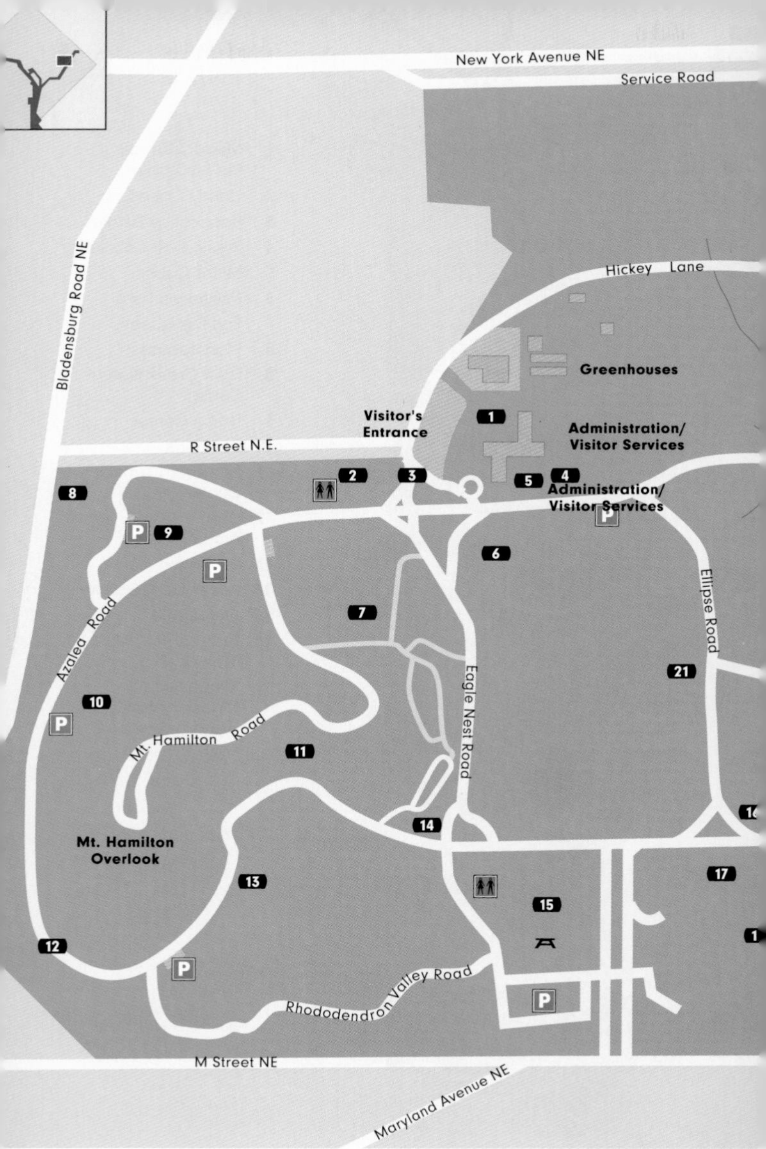

New York Avenue NE

Service Road

Hickey Lane

Greenhouses

Visitor's Entrance

1

Administration/ Visitor Services

R Street N.E.

2

3

5 4

Administration/ Visitor Services

8

P 9

P

6

7

Azalea Road

P 10

Mt. Hamilton Road

11

Ellipse Road

21

14

16

Mt. Hamilton Overlook

13

15

17

12

P

Rhododendron Valley Road

P

1

M Street NE

Maryland Avenue NE

Bladensburg Road NE

Eagle Nest Road

Listed by Site Number

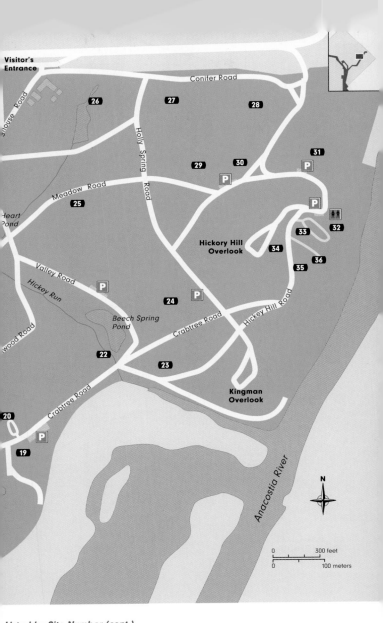

Visitor's Entrance

Conifer Road

26

27

28

Holly Spring Road

29

30

31

P

Meadow Road

25

P

Heart Pond

33

P

32

Hickory Hill Overlook

34

36

35

Valley Road

Hickey Run

P

24

P

Crabtree Road

Beech Spring Pond

Hickey Hill Road

22

23

Kingman Overlook

wood Road

Crabtree Road

20

P

19

Anacostia River

N

0   300 feet
0   100 meters

Listed by Site Number (cont.)

20 Fern Valley/ Native Plants

21 National Capitol Columns

22 Beech Pond Gazebo

23 Crab Apples

24 Holly and Magnolia Collections

25 Crape Myrtles

26 Maples

27 Japanese Maples

28 Dwarf Conifer Collection

29 Gotelli and Watnong Conifer Collection

30 Dawn Redwoods

31 Dogwood Collection

32 Japanese Woodland

33 Chadwick Overlook

34 Korean Hillside

35 China Valley

36 Garden Club Pagoda

SEE DETAIL MAP
OPPOSITE

Swains Lock (Lock 21)

Great Falls Park Visitor Center

Great Falls Tavern Visitor Center

Great Falls
Park

Falls Rd.

189

River Rd.

Maryland Gold Mine
site

190

Old Angler's Inn

Old Dominion Dr.

738

193

MARYLAND

495

MacArthur Blvd.

Carderock

Capital Beltway

495

Lock 14
Lock 13   Lock 12
Lock 11

Seven
Locks

Lock 10
Lock 9
Lock 8

Washington Dulles Access and Toll Rd.

Georgetown Pike

George Washington Memorial Pkwy.

Clara Barton National
Historic Site

267

Dolley

Madison

Blvd.

123

McLEAN

Glen Echo Park
Lock 7

BETHESDA

396

VIRGINIA

Old Dominion Dr.

Chain Bridge Rd.

George Washington
Memorial Parkway

Little Falls Dam

River Rd.

309

Lock 6

Lock 5

Little
Falls

Lee Hwy.

ARLINGTON

Chain Bridge

MacArthur Blvd.

Massachusetts Ave.

Wisconsin Ave.

29

66

Lee Hwy.

Abner Cloud House
Fletcher's Boathouse

Canal Rd.

DISTRICT OF COLUMBIA

50

Lee Hwy.

Georgetown
Reservoir

Rock Creek
Park

Potomac River

GEORGETOWN

Key Bridge

50

Arlington Blvd.

Locks
1-4

Georgetown
Visitor Center

New Hampshire Ave.

27

0   1 mile
0   1 km

N

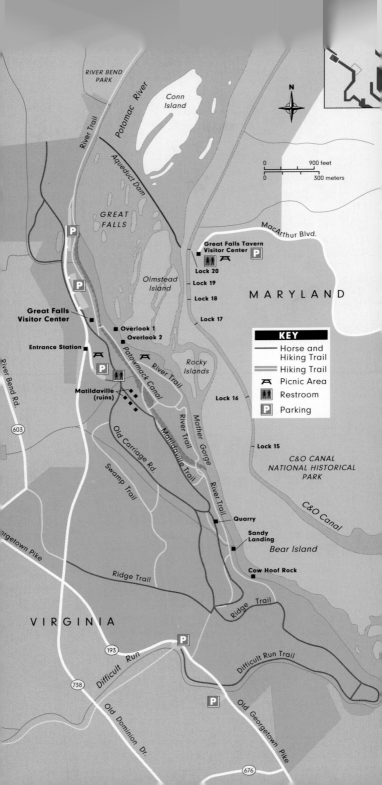

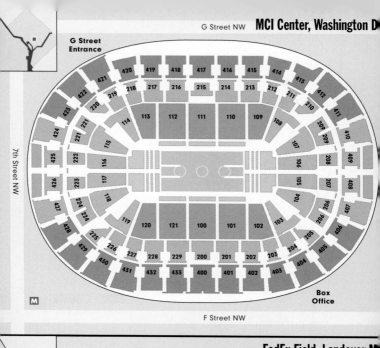

MCI Center, Washington D

G Street NW

G Street Entrance

7th Street NW

Box Office

F Street NW

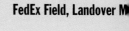

FedEx Field, Landover M

Oriole Park at Camden Yards, Baltimore MD

Patriot Center, Fairfax VA

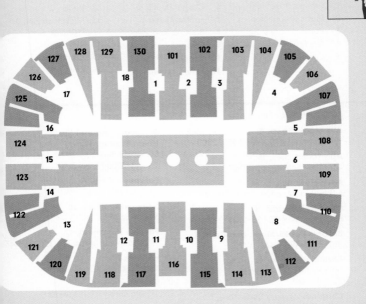

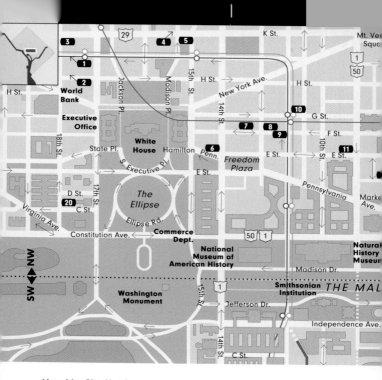

Listed by Site Number

1	Filene's Basement	**6**	Chanel Boutique	**12**	Vega
2	Music Box Center	**7**	Fahrney's Pens	**13**	Mickelson Fine Art Framing
3	Borders Books	**8**	Banana Republic	**14**	ROSExpress
4	Al's Magic Shop	**9**	Olsson's	**15**	Artifactory
5	Chapters	**10**	Hecht's	**15**	Kinko's
		11	Penn Camera		

Listed Alphabetically

Al's Magic Shop, 4.
1012 Vermont Ave NW ☎ 789–2800

Apartment Zero, 18.
406 7th St NW ☎ 628–4067

Artifactory, 15.
641 Indiana Ave NW ☎ 393–2727

Banana Republic, 8.
601 13th St NW ☎ 638–2724

Borders Books/Music and Cafe, 3.
1801 K St NW ☎ 466–4999

Chanel Boutique, 6.
1455 Pennsylvania Ave NW
☎ 638–5055

Chapters Literary Bookstore, 5.
1512 K St NW ☎ 347–5495

Discovery Channel Store - Union Station, 19.
50 Massachusetts Ave NE
☎ 842–3700

Fahrney's Pens, 7.
1317 F St NW ☎ 628–9525

Fairy Godmother, 20.
319 7th St SE ☎ 547–5474

Filene's Basement, 1.
1133 Connecticut Ave NW ☎ 872–8430

Hecht's, 10.
1201 G St NW ☎ 628–6661

Illuminations, 17.
415 8th St NW ☎ 783–4888

Listed by Site Number (cont.)

16 Pua Naturally
17 Illuminations
17 Teaism Tea Shop
18 Olsson's
18 Apartment Zero

19 Discovery Channel
    Store
20 Indian Craft Shop
21 Fairy Godmother

Listed Alphabetically (cont.)

Indian Craft Shop, 20. 1849 C St NW
(Dept of the Interior, Rm 1023)
☎ 208-4056

Kinko's, 15.
325 7th St NW ☎ 544-4796

Mickelson Fine Art Framing, 13.
629 New York Ave NW ☎ 628-1734

Music Box Center, 2.
1920 I St NW ☎ 783-9399

Olsson's Books and Records, 9.
1200 F St NW ☎ 347-3686

Olsson's Books and Records, 18.
416 7th St NW ☎ 638-7610

Penn Camera, 11.
840 E St NW ☎ 347-5777

Political Americana, 8. 1331
Pennsylvania Ave NW ☎ 737-7730

Pua Naturally, 16.
444 7th St NW ☎ 347-4543

ROSExpress, 14.
200 K St NW ☎ 842-1000

Teaism Tea Shop, 17.
400 8th St NW ☎ 638-7740

Vega, 12.
819 7th St NW ☎ 589-0140

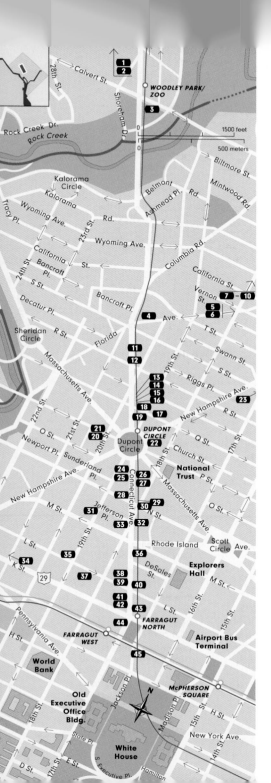

Listed by Site Number

1 Politics & Prose
2 Made By You
3 Antiques Anonymous
4 Newsroom
5 Millennium
6 Sisterspace
7 Skynear and Co
8 Chenonceau Antiques
9 Shake Your Booty
10 DC-CD
11 Secondi
12 Left Bank
13 Lambda Rising
14 Coffee & the Works
15 Melody Record Shop
16 Toast & Strawberries
17 Dupont Flowers
18 Kramer Book Store
19 Beadazzled
20 Second Story Books
21 The Third Day
22 Books A Million
23 Tapeheadz Video
24 Propper Topper
25 Betsy Fisher
26 Written Word
27 Card Gallery
28 Olsson's Books & Records
29 Copenhaver
30 Pampillonia
31 Jos A Bank Clothiers
32 Talbots
33 Kid's Closet
34 Reiter's Books
35 Abacus
36 Burberrys
37 Church's Shoes
38 Filene's Basement
39 Rizik Bros Inc
40 Tiny Jewel Box
41 Chocolate Chocolate
41 Victoria's Secret
42 Parade of Shoes
43 Custom Shop Shirtmakers
44 Nine West
45 The Map Store

Listed Alphabetically

Abacus Enterprise, 35.
1900 L St NW ☎ 775-9012

Antiques Anonymous, 2. 2627
Connecticut Ave NW ☎ 332-5555

Beadazzled, 19. 1507 Connecticut
Ave NW ☎ 265-2323

Betsy Fisher, 25. 1224 Connecticut
Ave NW ☎ 785-1975

Books A Million, 22.
11 Dupont Cir NW ☎ 319-1374

Burberrys, 36. 1155 Connecticut Ave NW
☎ 463-3000

Card Gallery, 27.
1363 Connecticut Ave NW ☎ 223-9230

Chenonceau Antiques, 8.
2314 18th St NW ☎ 667-1651

Chocolate Chocolate, 41.
1050 Connecticut Ave NW
☎ 466-2190

Church's English Shoes, 37.
1820 L St NW ☎ 296-3366

Coffee & the Works, 14. 1627
Connecticut Ave NW ☎ 483-8050

Copenhaver, 29.
1301 Connecticut Ave NW
☎ 232-1200

Custom Shop Shirtmakers, 43. 1033
Connecticut Ave NW ☎ 659-8250

DC-CD, 10. 2423 18th St NW
☎ 588-1810

Dupont Flowers, 17. 1900 Q St NW
☎ 797-7600

Filene's Basement, 38.
1130 Connecticut Ave NW ☎ 872-8430

Jos A Bank Clothiers, 31.
1200 19th St NW ☎ 466-2282

Kid's Closet, 33. 1226 Connecticut Ave
NW ☎ 429-9247

Kramerbooks, 18. 1517 Connecticut
Ave NW ☎ 387-1400

Lambda Rising, 13. 1625 Connecticut
Ave NW ☎ 462-6969

Left Bank, 12. 1627 Connecticut Ave
NW ☎ 518-4000

Made By You, 2. 3413 Connecticut
Ave NW ☎ 363-9590

The Map Store, 45. 1636 I St NW
☎ 628-2608

Melody Record Shop, 15.
1623 Connecticut Ave NW
☎ 232-4002

Millennium, 5. 1528 U St NW
☎ 462-4444

Newsroom, 4. 1753 Connecticut
Ave NW ☎ 332-1489

Nine West, 44. 1008 Connecticut Ave
NW ☎ 452-9163

Olsson's Books & Records, 28.
1307 19th St NW ☎ 785-1133

Pampillonia, 30. 1213 Connecticut
Ave NW ☎ 628-6305

Parade of Shoes, 42.
1020 Connecticut Ave NW
☎ 872-8581

Politics & Prose, 1.
5015 Connecticut Ave NW
☎ 364-1919

Propper Topper, 24.
1350 Connecticut Ave NW
☎ 842-3055

**Reiter's Scientific and
Professional Books, 34.**
2021 K St NW ☎ 223-3327

Rizik Bros Inc, 39.
1100 Connecticut Ave NW
☎ 223-4050

Second Story Books, 20.
2000 P St NW ☎ 659-8884

Secondi, 11. 1611 Connecticut Ave NW
☎ 667-1122

Shake Your Booty, 9. 2439 18th St NW
☎ 518-8205

Sisterspace, 6. 1515 U St NW
☎ 332-3443

Skynear and Co., 7.
1800 Wyoming Ave NW ☎ 797-7160

Talbots, 32. 1122 Connecticut Ave NW
☎ 887-6973

Tapeheadz Video, 23.
1709 17th St NW ☎ 234-5590

The Third Day, 21.
2001 P St NW ☎ 785-0107

Tiny Jewel Box, 40. 1147 Connecticut
Ave NW ☎ 393-2747

Toast & Strawberries, 16.
1608 20th St NW ☎ 234-2424

Victoria's Secret, 41.
1050 Connecticut Ave NW
☎ 293-7530

Written Word, 26.
1365 Connecticut Ave NW
☎ 223-1400

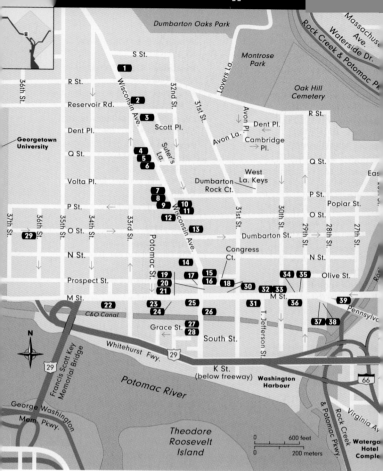

Listed by Site Number

1 Miller & Arney Antiques
2 A Mano
3 Sugar
4 Piccolo Piggies
5 Cherry
5 Phoenix
7 Commander Salamander
8 Beyond Comics 2
9 Balaquin
10 Little Caledonia
11 Appalachian Spring
12 Armani Exchange
13 Betsey Johnson
14 The Gap
15 Diesel

16 Hats in the Belfry
17 Restoration Hardware
18 Booked Up
19 Smith & Hawken
20 Coach Store
21 Benetton
22 Ann Sacks Tile & Stone
23 Dean & DeLuca
24 Abercrombie
24 Ann Taylor Loft
24 Crabtree & Evelyn
24 J Crew
24 Platypus
24 Polo/Ralph Lauren
24 Victoria's Secret

25 Banana Republic
26 Pleasure Place
27 Peace Frogs
28 Patagonia
29 Susquehanna
30 Urban Outfitters
31 Barnes & Noble
32 Pottery Barn
33 Bartleby's Books
34 Keith Lipert Gallery
35 Cherub Antiques Gallery
36 The American Studio
37 Justine Mehlman Antiques
38 Lorenzodonna
39 Bridge Street Books

Listed Alphabetically

Abercrombie , 24.
1208 Wisconsin Ave NW ☎ 333-1566

A Mano, 2. 1677 Wisconsin Ave NW
☎ 298-7200

The American Studio, 36. 2906 M St NW
☎ 965-3273

Ann Sacks Tile & Stone, 22.
3328 M St NW ☎ 339-0840

Ann Taylor Loft, 24. 3265 M St NW
☎ 625-7527

Appalachian Spring, 11.
1415 Wisconsin Ave NW
☎ 337-5780

Armani Exchange, 12
1254 Wisconsin Ave NW
☎ 965-9820

Balaquin, 9. 1413 Wisconsin Ave NW
☎ 625-1600

Banana Republic, 25. 3200 M St NW
☎ 333-2554

Barnes & Noble, 31. 3040 M St NW
☎ 965-9880

Bartleby's Books, 33. 3034 M St NW
☎ 298-0486

Benetton, 21. 1200 Wisconsin Ave NW
☎ 625-0443

Betsey Johnson, 13. 1321 Wisconsin
Ave NW ☎ 338-4090

Beyond Comics 2, 8.
1419 Wisconsin Ave NW ☎ 333-8651

Booked Up, 18. 1204 31st St NW
☎ 965-3244

Bridge Street Books, 39. 2814
Pennsylvania Ave NW ☎ 965-5200

Cherry, 5. 1526 Wisconsin Ave NW
☎ 342-3600

Cherub Antiques Gallery, 35.
2918 M St NW ☎ 337-2224

Coach Store, 20. 3259 M St NW
☎ 333-3005

Commander Salamander, 7. 1420
Wisconsin Ave NW ☎ 337-2265

Crabtree & Evelyn, 24. 3222 M St NW
☎ 342-1934

Dean & DeLuca, 23. 3276 M St NW
☎ 342-2500

Diesel, 15. 1249 Wisconsin Ave NW
☎ 625-2780

The Gap, 14. 1258 Wisconsin Ave NW
☎ 333-2657

Hats in the Belfry, 16.
1250 Wisconsin Ave NW ☎ 342-2006

J Crew, 24. 3222 M St NW
☎ 965-4090

Justine Mehlman Antiques, 37,
2824 Pennsylvania Ave NW
☎ 337-0613

Keith Lipert Gallery, 34. 2922 M St
NW ☎ 965-9736

Little Caledonia, 10.
1419 Wisconsin Ave NW ☎ 333-4700

Lorenzodonna, 38. 2822 Pennsylvania
Ave NW ☎ 337-0622

Miller & Arney Antiques, 1.
1737 Wisconsin Ave NW ☎ 338-2369

Patagonia, 28. 1048 Wisconsin Ave
NW ☎ 333-1776

Peace Frogs of Georgetown, 27.
1073 Wisconsin Ave NW ☎ 298-7663

Phoenix, 5. 1514 Wisconsin Ave NW
☎ 338-4404

Piccolo Piggies, 4.
1533 Wisconsin Ave NW ☎ 333-0123

Platypus, 24. 3222 M St NW
☎ 338-7680

Pleasure Place, 26.
1063 Wisconsin Ave NW ☎ 333-8570

Polo/Ralph Lauren, 24. 3222 M St NW
☎ 965-0904

Pottery Barn, 32. 3077 M St NW
☎ 337-8900

Restoration Hardware, 17.
1222 Wisconsin Ave NW ☎ 625-2771

Smith & Hawken, 19. 1209 31st St NW
☎ 965-2680

Sugar, 3. 1633 Wisconsin Ave NW
☎ 333-5331

Susquehanna, 29. 3612 O St NW
☎ 333-1511

Urban Outfitters, 30. 3111 M St NW
☎ 342-1012

Victoria's Secret, 24. 3222 M St NW
☎ 965-5457

Listed Alphabetically

Ballston Commons, 17.
☎ 703/243-8088

Chevy Chase Pavilion, 5.
☎ 686-5335

City Place, 4. ☎ 301/589-1091

Dupont Circle Area, 9.

Eastern Market, 14.

Fair Oaks Mall, 20. ☎ 703/359-8300

Fashion Centre, 15. ☎ 703/415-2400

Georgetown Park, 10. ☎ 298-5577

Iverson Mall, 8. ☎ 301/423-7400

Lakeforest Shopping Center, 1.
☎ 301/840-5840

Landmark Mall, 21. ☎ 703/941-2582

Mazza Gallerie, 6. ☎ 966-6114

Old Post Office Pavilion, 12.
☎ 289-4224

Pentagon Row, 16. ☎ 703/418-6666

Listed Alphabetically (cont.)

Potomac Mills Mall, 23.
☎ 703/490–5948

Prince George's Plaza, 7.
☎ 301/559–8844

The Shops at National Place, 11.
☎ 662–1250

Springfield Mall, 22. ☎ 703/971–3000

Tysons Corner Center, 19.
☎ 703/847–7300

Tyson's Galleria, 18. ☎ 703/827–7700

Union Station, 13. ☎ 371–9441

**Westfield Shoppingtown
Montgomery, 3.** ☎ 301/469–6000

White Flint, 2. ☎ 301/468–5777

Listed by Site Number

1 Cashion's Eats Place
2 Perry's
3 Grill from Ipanema
4 Churerria Madrid
5 Mixtec
6 Pasta Mia
7 Red Sea
8 La Fourchette
9 Meskerem
10 Cities
11 Felix
12 Bukom Cafe
13 Bardia's New Orleans
14 Little Fountain Cafe
15 Saigonnais
16 Florida Ave Grill
17 Addis Ababa
18 Julia's Empanadas
19 Kuna
20 Utopia
21 Coppi's Pizza
22 Polly's Café
23 Ben's Chili Bowl
24 The Islander
25 Wazuri
26 Ruth's Chris Steakhouse
27 Lauriol Plaza
28 Himalayan Grill
29 Anna Maria's
30 Timberlake's
31 City Lights of China
32 Teaism
33 Odeon Cafe
34 La Tomate
35 Nora
36 Townhouse Tavern
37 Childe Harold
38 Etrusco
39 Raku
40 Mercury Grill
41 Peppers
41 Trio Restaurant
42 Cafe Luna
42 Skewers
43 Obelisk
43 Pizza Paradiso
44 Johnny's Half Shell
45 Gabriel
46 Be Du Ci
47 Cafe Japone

48 Pan Asian Noodles & Grill
49 Pesce
50 Sala Thai
51 Front Page
52 Cafe Citron
53 Luna Grill
54 The Melting Pot
55 Firefly
56 The Colonnade
57 Melrose
58 Blackie's House of Beef
59 Circle Bistro
60 Marcel's
61 Dish
62 Roof Terrace
63 Grillfish
64 Galileo
65 i Ricchi
66 Fin
66 Sam & Harry's
67 Vidalia
68 Palm
69 Bacchus
70 Star of Siam
71 Luigi's
72 Oodles Noodles
73 Mr K's
74 Tequila Grill
74 Thai Kingdom
75 Prime Rib
75 Legal Sea Foods
76 El Chalan
77 Primi Piatti
78 Kinkead's
79 Taberna Del Alabardero
80 Tabard Inn
81 Iron Gate Inn
82 Dragonfly
83 Cafe Promenade
84 Ascot
85 Fran O'Brien's Steak House
86 Bombay Club
87 Equinox
88 Olive's
89 Gerard's Place
90 Georgia Brown's
91 Mar de Plata
92 Hamburger Mary's
93 DC Coast

94 Isabella
95 Cafe 15
96 Benkay
97 Tuscana West
98 Morrison-Clark Inn
99 Coeur de Lion
100 Capital City Brewing Co
100 Haad Thai
100 Luigino
101 Old Ebbitt Grille
102 Occidental
103 Red Sage
104 M & S Grill
105 ESPN Zone
106 Les Halles
107 Jordan's
108 Friday's
109 Ten Penh
110 Zaytinya
111 Marrakesh
112 Tony Cheng's
113 Li Ho Food
114 Full Kee
115 Hunan's Chinatown
116 Hard Rock Cafe
117 Café Atlántico
118 Austin Grill
119 Jaleo
120 701 Pennsylvania
121 District Chophouse & Brewery
122 Nick & Stef's
123 Burma
124 Cafe Asia

Listed Alphabetically

Addis Ababa, 17. 2106 18th St NW
☎ 232-6092. Ethiopian. $$$

Anna Maria's, 29.
1737 Connecticut Ave NW
☎ 667-1444. Italian. $$

Ascot, 84. 1708 L St NW
☎ 296-7640. Continental. $$

Austin Grill, 118. 750 E St NW
☎ 393-3776. Tex-Mex. $$

Bacchus, 69. 1827 Jefferson Pl NW
☎ 785-0734. Middle Eastern. $$

Bardia's New Orleans, 13.
2412 18th St NW ☎ 234-0420.
Creole/Cajun. $

Be Du Ci, 46. 2100 P NW
☎ 223-3824. Mediterranean. $$$

Benkay, 96. 727 15th St NW
☎ 737-1515. Japanese. $

Ben's Chili Bowl, 23. 1213 U St NW
☎ 667-0909. American. $

Blackie's House of Beef, 58.
1217 22nd St NW ☎ 333-1100.
American. $$

Bombay Club, 86. 815 Connecticut
Ave NW ☎ 659-3727. Indian. $$$

Bukom Cafe, 12. 2442 18th St NW
☎ 265-4600. African. $$

Burma, 123. 740 6th St NW
☎ 638-1280. Asian. $$

Cafe Asia, 124. 1720 I St NW
☎ 659-2696. Asian. $

Café Atlántico, 117. 405 8th St NW
☎ 393-0812. New Latin. $$$

Cafe Citron, 52. 1343 Connecticut Ave
NW ☎ 530-8844. Mexican. $

Cafe 15, 95. 806 15th St NW
☎ 730-8800. French. $$$

Cafe Japone, 47. 2032 P St NW
☎ 223-1573. Japanese. $$-$$$

Cafe Luna, 42. 1633 P St NW
☎ 387-4005. American. $

Cafe Promenade, 83.
1127 Connecticut Ave NW
☎ 347-2233. Mediterranean. $$

Capital City Brewing Co, 100.
1100 New York Ave NW
☎ 628-2222. American. $$

Cashion's Eat Place, 1.
1819 Columbia Rd NW
☎ 797-1819. Continental. $$$

Childe Harold, 37. 1610 20th St
NW ☎ 483-6700. American. $$

Churerria Madrid, 4.
2505 Champlain St NW ☎ 483-4441.
Spanish. $

Circle Bistro, 53.
1 Washington Circle NW
☎ 293-5390. International. $$$

Cities, 10. 2424 18th St NW
☎ 328-7194. Continental. $$$

City Lights of China, 31.
1731 Connecticut Ave NW
☎ 265-6688. Chinese. $$

Coeur de Lion, 99.
926 Massachusetts Ave NW
☎ 414-0500. Continental. $$$

The Colonnade, 56. 2401 M St NW
☎ 457-5000. Continental. $$$$

Coppi's Pizza, 21. 1414 U St NW
☎ 319-7773. Italian. $$

DC Coast, 93. 1401 K St NW
☎ 216-5988. Contemporary. $$$$

Dish, 61. 924 25th St NW
☎ 338-8707. American. $$

District Chophouse & Brewery, 121.
509 7th St NW ☎ 347-3434.
American. $$

Dragonfly, 82. 1215 Connecticut Ave
NW☎ 331-1775. Japanese. $$

El Chalan, 76. 1924 I St NW
☎ 293-2765. S. American. $$

Equinox, 87. 818 Connecticut Ave NW
☎ 331-8118. Contemporary. $$

ESPN Zone, 105. 555 12th St NW
☎ 783-3776. American. $$

Etrusco, 38. 1606 20th St NW
☎ 667-0047. Italian. $$

Felix, 11. 2406 18th St NW
☎ 483-3549. New American. $$$

Fin, 66. 1200 19th St NW ☎ 530-4430.
Seafood. $$

Firefly, 55. 1310 New Hampshire Ave
NW ☎ 861-1310. American. $$

Florida Ave Grill, 16. 1100 Florida
Ave NW ☎ 265-1586. Soul Food. $

Fran O'Brien's Steak House, 85.
1001 16th St ☎ 783-2599.
American. $$$

$$$$ = over $35 $$$ = $25-$35 $$ = $15-$25 $ = under $15
Based on cost per person, excluding drinks, service, and 9% sales tax.

Listed Alphabetically (cont.)

Front Page, 51. 1333 New Hampshire Ave NW ☎ 296–6500. American. $$

Full Kee, 114. 509 H St NW ☎ 371–2233. Chinese. $$

Gabriel, 45. 2121 P St NW ☎ 956–6690. Spanish. $$$

Galileo, 64. 1110 21st St NW ☎ 293–7191. Italian. $$$$

Georgia Brown's, 90. 950 15th St NW ☎ 393–4499. Southern. $$

Gerard's Place, 89. 915 15th St NW ☎ 737–4445. French. $$$$

Grill from Ipanema, 3. 1858 Columbia Rd ☎ 986–0757. Brazilian. $$

Grillfish, 63. 1200 New Hampshire NW ☎ 331–7310. Seafood. $$

Haad Thai, 100. 1100 New York Ave NW ☎ 682–1111. Thai. $$

Hamburger Mary's, 92. 1337 14th St NW ☎ 232–7010. Burgers. $

Hard Rock Cafe, 116. 999 E St NW ☎ 737–7625. American. $$

Himalayan Grill, 28. 1805 18th St NW ☎ 986–5124. Indian. $

Hunan Chinatown, 115. 624 H St NW ☎ 783–5858. Chinese. $$

i Ricchi, 65. 1220 19th St NW ☎ 835–0459. Italian. $$$$

Iron Gate Inn, 81. 1734 N St NW ☎ 737–1370. Mediterranean. $$

Isabella, 94. 809 15th St NW ☎ 408–9500. Mediterranean. $$

The Islander, 24. 1201 U St NW ☎ 234–4955. Caribbean. $

Jaleo, 119. 480 7th St NW ☎ 628–7949. Spanish. $$

Johnny's Half Shell, 44. 2002 P St NW ☎ 296–2021. Seafood. $$$

Jordan's, 107. 1300 Pennsylvania Ave NW ☎ 589–1223. American. $$$

Julia's Empanadas, 18. 1410 U St NW ☎ 387–4100. S. American. $

Kinkead's, 78. 2000 Pennsylvania Ave NW ☎ 296–7700. Seafood. $$$$

Kuna, 19. 1324 U St NW ☎ 797–7908. E. European. $$

La Fourchette, 8. 2429 18th St NW ☎ 332–3077. French. $$

La Tomate, 34. 1701 Connecticut Ave NW ☎ 667–5505. Italian. $$$

Lauriol Plaza, 27. 1835 18th St NW ☎ 387–0035. Southwestern. $$

Legal Sea Foods, 75. 2020 K St NW ☎ 496–1111. Seafood. $$

Les Halles, 106. 1201 Pennsylvania Ave NW ☎ 347–6848. French. $$$$

Li Ho Food, 113. 501 H St NW ☎ 289–2059. Szechuan. $$

Little Fountain Cafe, 14. 2339 18th St NW ☎ 462–8100. American Bistro. $$

Luigino, 100. 1100 New York Ave NW ☎ 371–0595. Italian. $$

Luigi's, 71. 1132 19th St NW ☎ 331–7574. Italian. $$

Luna Grill, 53. 1301 Connecticut Ave NW ☎ 835–2280. American. $

M & S Grill, 104. 600 13th St NW ☎ 347–1500. Steakhouse. $$

Mar de Plata, 91. 1410 14th St NW ☎ 234–2679. Latin American. $$

Marcel's, 60. 2401 Pennsylvania Ave NW ☎ 296–1166. Belgian. $$$

Marrakesh, 111. 617 New York Ave NW ☎ 393–9393. Moroccan. $$

Melrose, 57. 1201 24th St NW ☎ 419–6755. American. $$$

The Melting Pot, 54. 1220 19th St NW ☎ 857–0777. Fondue. $$$

Mercury Grill, 40. 1602 17th St NW ☎ 667–5937. New American. $$

Meskerem, 9. 2434 18th St NW ☎ 462–4100. Ethiopian. $

Mixtec, 5. 1792 Columbia Rd NW ☎ 332–1011. Mexican. $$

Morrison-Clark Inn, 98. 1015 L St NW ☎ 898–1200. American. $$$$

Mr K's, 73. 2121 K St NW ☎ 331–8868. Chinese. $$$$

Nick & Stef's, 122. 601 F St NW ☎ 661–5040. Steakhouse. $$$

Nora, 35. 2132 Florida Ave NW ☎ 462–5143. Organic. $$$$

Obelisk, 43. 2029 P St NW ☎ 872–1180. Italian. $$$$

Occidental Grill, 102. 1475 Pennsylvania Ave NW ☎ 783–1475. American. $$$

Odeon Cafe, 33. 1714 Connecticut Ave NW ☎ 328-6228. Italian. $$

Old Ebbitt Grill, 101. 675 15th St NW ☎ 347-4800. American. $$$

Olive's, 88. 1600 K St NW ☎ 452-1886. Italian. $$$

Oodles Noodles, 72. 1120 19th St NW ☎ 293-3138. Asian. $

Palm, 68. 1225 19th St NW ☎ 293-9091. American. $$$$

Pan Asian Noodles & Grill, 43. 2020 P St NW ☎ 872-8889. Thai. $

Pasta Mia, 6. 1790 Columbia Rd NW ☎ 328-9114. Italian. $

Peppers, 41. 1527 17th St NW ☎ 328-8193. Southwest. $

Perry's, 2. 1811 Columbia Rd NW ☎ 234-6218. Japanese. $$

Pesce, 49. 2016 P St NW ☎ 466-3474. Seafood. $$$

Pizza Paradiso, 43. 2029 P St NW ☎ 223-1245. Italian. $$

Polly's Café, 22. 1342 U St NW ☎ 265-8385. American. $$

Prime Rib, 75. 2020 K St NW ☎ 466-8811. American. $$$$

Primi Piatti, 77. 2013 I St NW ☎ 223-3600. Italian. $$

Raku, 39. 1900 Q St NW ☎ 265-7258. Asian. $$

Red Sage, 103. 605 14th St NW ☎ 638-4444. Southwestern. $$$

Red Sea, 7. 2463 18th St NW ☎ 483-5000. Ethiopian. $

Roof Terrace, 62. Kennedy Center NW ☎ 416-8555. American. $$$

Ruth's Chris Steakhouse, 26. 1801 Connecticut Ave NW ☎ 797-0033. Steakhouse. $$$

Saigonnais, 15. 2307 18th St NW ☎ 232-5300. Asian. $$

Sala Thai, 50. 2016 P St NW ☎ 872-1144. Thai. $$$

Sam & Harry's, 66. 1200 19th St NW ☎ 296-4333. American. $$$$

701 Pennsylvania, 120. 701 Pennsylvania Ave NW ☎ 393-0701. American. $$$$

Skewers, 42. 1633 P St NW ☎ 387-7400. Middle Eastern. $$

Star of Siam, 70. 1136 19th St NW ☎ 785-2839. Thai. $$

Tabard Inn, 80. 1739 N St NW ☎ 785-1277. American. $$$$

Taberna del Alabardero, 79. 1776 I St NW ☎ 429-2200. Spanish. $$$

Teaism, 32. 2009 R St NW ☎ 667-3827. Pan-Asian. $$

Ten Penh, 109. 1001 Pennsylvania Ave NW ☎ 393-4500. Asian. $$

Tequila Grill, 74. 1990 K St NW ☎ 833-3640. Southwestern. $

TGI Friday's, 108. 1201 Pennsylvania Ave NW ☎ 628-8443. American. $

Thai Kingdom, 74. 2021 K St NW ☎ 835-1700. Thai. $

Timberlake's, 30. 1726 Connecticut Ave NW ☎ 483-2266. American. $

Tony Cheng's, 112. 621 H St NW ☎ 371-8669. Mongolian. $$

Townhouse Tavern, 36. 1637 R St NW ☎ 234-5747. American. $$

Trio Restaurant, 41. 1537 17th St NW ☎ 232-6505. American. $

Tuscana West, 97. 1350 I St NW ☎ 289-7300. Italian. $$

Utopia, 20. 1418 U St NW ☎ 483-7669. International. $$$

Vidalia, 67. 1990 M St NW ☎ 659-1990. American. $$$$

Wazuri, 25. 1836 18th St NW ☎ 797-4930. African. $$

Zaytinya, 110. 701 9th St NW ☎ 638-0800. Greek/Mediterranean. $$

$$$$ = over $35 $$$ = $25-$35 $$ = $15-$25 $ = under $15
Based on cost per person, excluding drinks, service, and 9% sales tax.

Listed by Site Number

1	America	**12**	White Tiger	**26**	Burrito Brothers
1	B. Smith's	**13**	Armands Pizzeria	**27**	Tune Inn
1	Johnny Rockets	**14**	Two Quail	**28**	Hawk & Dove
1	Pizzeria Uno	**15**	Café Berlin	**29**	Market Lunch
1	Thunder Grill	**16**	La Loma	**30**	Mr Henry's
2	Capital City Brewing Co	**17**	French's Fine Southern Cuisine	**31**	Aatish
3	Dubliner	**18**	Horace & Dickie's Seafood	**32**	Anatolia
4	Kelly's Irish Times			**33**	Bread & Chocolate
5	Bistro Bis	**19**	Philips Flagship	**34**	Monmartre
6	Capitol View Club	**20**	Pier 7	**35**	Banana Cafe
7	La Colline	**21**	GangPlank Marina	**36**	Trattoria Alberto
8	Capital Grille	**22**	Tortilla Coast Marina		
9	Charlie Palmer Steak	**23**	Bullfeathers		
10	Monocle	**24**	Barolo		
11	La Brasserie	**24**	Il Radicchio's		
		25	Hunan Dynasty		

Listed Alphabetically

Aatish, 31. 609 Pennsylvania Ave SE ☎ 544-0931. Indian/Pakistani. $$

America, 1. 50 Massachusetts Ave NE ☎ 682-9555. American. $

Anatolia, 32. 633 Pennsylvania Ave SE ☎ 544-4753. Turkish. $$

Armands Pizzeria, 13. 226 Massachusetts Ave NE ☎ 547-6600. Italian. $

B. Smith's, 1. 50 Massachusetts Ave NE ☎ 289-6188. American. $$

Banana Cafe, 35. 500 8th St SE ☎ 543-5906. Latin. $$

Barolo, 24. 223 Pennsylvania Ave SE ☎ 547-5011. American. $$$

Bistro Bis (Hotel George), 5. 15 E St NW ☎ 661-2700. American/French. $$$

Bread & Chocolate, 34. 666 Pennsylvania Ave SE ☎ 547-2875. French. $

Bullfeathers, 23. 410 1st St SE ☎ 543-5005. American. $

Burrito Brothers, 26. 205 Pennsylvania Ave SE ☎ 543-6835. Mexican. $

Café Berlin, 15. 322 Massachusetts Ave NE ☎ 543-7656. German. $$

Capital City Brewing Co., 2. 2 Massachusetts Ave NE ☎ 842-2337. American. $$

Capital Grille, 8. 601 Pennsylvania Ave NW ☎ 737-6200. Steakhouse. $$$

Capitol View Club, 6. 400 New Jersey Ave NW ☎ 639-8439. American. $$

Charlie Palmer Steak, 9. 101 Constitution Ave NW ☎ 547-8100. Steakhouse. $$$

Dubliner, 3. 520 N Capitol St NW ☎ 737-3773. Irish. $

French's Fine Southern Cuisine, 17. 1365 H St NE ☎ 396-0991. Southern/Soul. $

GangPlank Marina, 21. 600 Water St SW ☎ 554-5000. Seafood. $$

Hawk & Dove, 28. 329 Pennsylvania Ave SE ☎ 543-3300. American. $

Horace & Dickie's Seafood, 18. 809 12th St NE ☎ 397-6040. African/Southern. $

Hunan Dynasty, 25. 215 Pennsylvania Ave SE ☎ 546-6161. Chinese. $

Il Radicchio's, 24. 223 Pennsylvania Ave SE ☎ 547-5114. Italian. $

Johnny Rocket's, 1. 50 Massachusetts Ave NE (Union Station) ☎ 289-6969. American. $

Kelly's Irish Times, 14. 14 F St NW ☎ 543-5433. Irish. $

La Brasserie, 11. 239 Massachusetts Ave NE ☎ 546-9154. French. $$$

La Colline, 7. 400 N Capitol St NW ☎ 737-0400. French. $$$

La Loma, 16. 316 Massachusetts Ave NE ☎ 548-2550. Mex/Tex-Mex. $

Market Lunch, 29. 225 7th St SE ☎ 547-8444. Seafood. $

Monocle, 9. 107 D St NE ☎ 546-4488. American. $$$

Monmartre, 34. 327 7th St SE ☎ 544-1244. French. $$

Mr. Henry's, 30. 601 Pennsylvania Ave SE ☎ 546-8412. American. $

Philips Flagship, 19. 900 Water St SW ☎ 488-8515. Seafood. $$$

Pier 7, 20. 650 Water St SW ☎ 554-2500. Continental. $$

Pizzeria Uno, 1. 50 Massachusetts Ave NE ☎ 842-0438. American. $$

Thunder Grill, 1. 50 Massachusetts Ave NE (Union Station) ☎ 898-0051. Tex-Mex. $

Tortilla Coast, 22. 400 1st St SE ☎ 546-6768. Mexican. $$

Trattoria Alberto, 36. 506 8th St SE ☎ 544-2007. Italian. $

Tune Inn, 27. 331½ Pennsylvania Ave SE ☎ 543-2725. American. $

Two Quail, 14. 320 Massachusetts Ave NE ☎ 543-8030. American/Seafood. $$

White Tiger, 12. 301 Massachusetts Ave NE ☎ 546-5900. Indian. $$

$$$$ = *over $35* $$$ = *$25-$35* $$ = *$15-$25* $ = *under $15*
Based on cost per person, excluding drinks, service, and 9% sales tax.

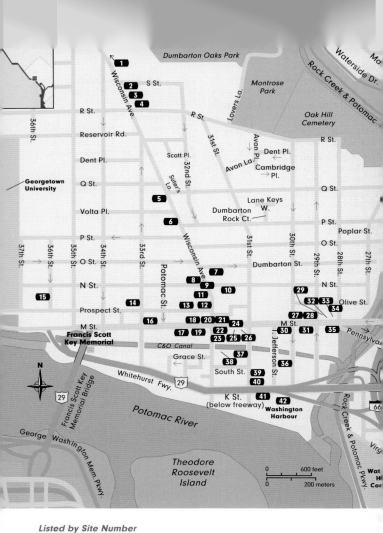

Listed by Site Number

1 Heritage India	**16** Amma Vegetarian Kitchen	**29** Mendocino Grille & Wine Bar
2 Cafe Divan	**17** Clyde's	**30** Citronelle
3 Acajutta	**18** Fettoosh	**31** Vietnam Georgetown
4 Japan Inn	**19** Samurai Japanese Steak & Seafood	**32** La Chaumière
5 Red Ginger	**20** Pizzeria Uno	**33** Enriqueta's
6 Bistrot Lepic	**21** Old Glory	**34** Zed's Ethiopian
7 Au Pied de Cochon	**22** Nathan's	**35** Seasons
8 Paolo's	**23** Ching Ching Cha	**36** Bake & Wired
9 Daily Grill	**23** Chopsticks	**37** Sea Catch
10 Neyla	**24** Mie N Yu	**38** Filomena's
11 Martin's Tavern	**25** Bistro Français	**39** Paper Moon
12 Third Edition	**26** Mr. Smith's	**40** Café La Ruche
13 Café Milano	**27** Garretts	**41** Sequoia
13 Morton's of Chicago	**28** The Guards	**42** Tony & Joe's
14 Aditi		
15 1789		

Acajutla, 3. 1721 Wisconsin Ave NW ☎ 965-9333. Latin American. $

Aditi, 14. 3299 M St NW ☎ 625-6825. Indian. $$

Amma Vegetarian Kitchen, 16. 3291-A M St NW ☎ 625-6625. $

Au Pied du Cochon, 7. 1335 Wisconsin Ave NW ☎ 337-6400. French. $

Bake & Wired, 36. 1052 Thomas Jefferson St ☎ 333-2500. Bakery. $

Bistro Français, 25. 3128 M St NW ☎ 338-3830. French. $$$

Bistrot Lepic, 6. 1736 Wisconsin Ave NW ☎ 331-0111. French. $$

Cafe Divan, 2. 1834 Wisconsin Ave NW ☎ 338-1747. Middle East. $$

Café La Ruche, 40. 1039 31st St NW ☎ 965-2684. French. $

Café Milano, 13. 3251 Prospect St NW ☎ 333-6183. Italian. $$$

Ching Ching Cha, 23. 1063 Wisconsin Ave NW ☎ 333-8288. Teahouse. $

Chopsticks, 23. 1073 Wisconsin Ave NW ☎ 338-6161. Japanese. $$

Citronelle, 30. 3000 M St NW (Latham Hotel) ☎ 625-2150. American. $$$$

Clyde's, 17. 3236 M St NW ☎ 333-9180. American. $$

Daily Grill, 9. 1310 Wisconsin Ave NW ☎ 337-4900. American. $$

Enriqueta's, 33. 2811 M St NW ☎ 338-7772. Mexican. $$

Fettoosh, 18. 3277 M St NW ☎ 342-1199. Lebanese. $$

Filomena's, 38. 1063 Wisconsin Ave NW ☎ 337-2782. Italian. $$

Garretts, 27. 3003 M St NW ☎ 333-8282. American. $

The Guards, 28. 2915 M St NW ☎ 965-2350. American. $$

Heritage India, 1. 2400 Wisconsin Ave NW ☎ 333-3120. Indian. $$

Japan Inn, 4. 1715 Wisconsin Ave NW ☎ 337-3400. Japanese. $$

La Chaumière, 32. 2813 M St NW ☎ 338-1784. French. $$$

Martin's Tavern, 11. 1264 Wisconsin Ave NW ☎ 333-7370. American. $

Mendocino Grille & Wine Bar, 29. 2917 M St NW ☎ 333-2912. American. $$

Mie N Yu, 24. 3125 M St NW ☎ 333-6122. Fusion. $$

Morton's of Chicago, 13. 3251 Prospect St NW ☎ 342-6258. Steakhouse. $$$$

Mr. Smith's, 21. 3104 M St NW ☎ 333-3104. American. $$

Nathan's, 22. 3150 M St NW ☎ 338-2000. Italian. $$$

Neyla, 10. 3206 N St NW ☎ 333-6353. Mediterranean. $$$

Old Glory, 21. 3139 M St NW ☎ 337-3406. BBQ. $$

Paolo's, 8. 1303 Wisconsin Ave NW ☎ 333-7353. Italian. $$$

Paper Moon, 39. 1073 31st St NW ☎ 965-6666. Italian. $$

Pizzeria Uno, 20. 3211 M St NW ☎ 965-6333. American. $

Red Ginger, 5. 1564 Wisconsin Ave NW ☎ 965-7009. Caribbean. $$

Samurai Japanese Steak & Seafood, 19. 3222 M St NW ☎ 333-1001. Japanese. $$

Sea Catch, 37. 1054 31 St NW ☎ 337-8855. Seafood. $$$

Seasons, 35. 2800 Pennsylvania Ave NW (Four Seasons Hotel) ☎ 944-2000. Continental. $$$$

Sequoia, 41. 3000 K St NW ☎ 944-4200. American. $$

1789, 15. 1226 36th St NW ☎ 965-1789. American. $$$$

Third Edition, 12. 1218 Wisconsin Ave NW ☎ 333-3700. American. $

Tony & Joe's, 42. 3050 K St NW ☎ 944-4545. Seafood. $$$

Vietnam Georgetown, 26. 2934 M St NW ☎ 337-4536. Vietnamese. $

Zed's Ethiopian Cuisine, 34. 1201 28th St NW ☎ 333-4710. Ethiopian. $

$$$$ = *over $35* $$$ = *$25-$35* $$ = *$15-$25* $ = *under $15*

Based on cost per person, excluding drinks, service, and 9% sales tax.

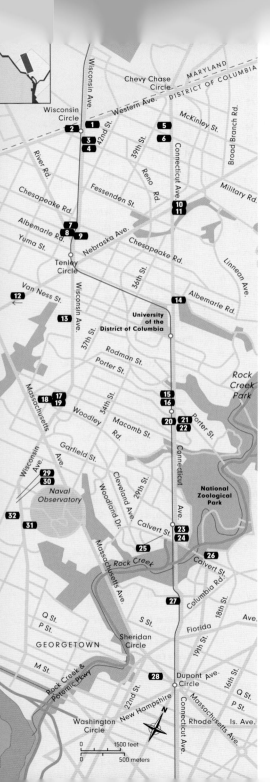

Listed by Site Number

1 Maggiano's Little Italy
2 Booeymonger
3 Chadwick's
4 Bambule
5 American City Diner
6 Parthenon
7 Yosaku
8 Caravela
9 Dancing Crab
9 Krupins Deli
10 Greenwood
11 Thai Room
12 Chef Geoff's
13 Cafe Ole
14 Shanghai Garden
15 Indique
16 Yanni's Greek Taverna
17 Cactus Cantina
18 2 Amys
19 Cafe Deluxe
20 Ireland's Four Provinces
21 Lavandou
22 Amernick
22 Ardeo
23 Thai Town
24 Lebanese Taverna
25 New Heights
26 Mama Ayesha's
27 Trocadero
28 Al Tiramisu
29 Old Europe
30 Austin Grill
31 Sushi-Ko
32 Busara

Listed Alphabetically

Al Tiramisu, 28. 2014 P St NW
☎ 467-4466. Italian. $$

American City Diner, 5.
5532 Connecticut Ave NW
☎ 244-1949. American. $

Amernick, 22. 3313 Connecticut Ave
NW ☎ 537-5855. Bakery. $

Ardeo, 22. 3311 Connecticut Ave NW
☎ 244-6750. New American. $$

Austin Grill, 30. 2404 Wisconsin Ave
NW ☎ 337-8080. Tex-Mex. $

Bambule, 4. 5225 Wisconsin Ave NW
☎ 966-0300. Mediterranean. $$

Booeymonger, 2.
5262 Wisconsin Ave NW
☎ 686-5805. Sandwiches. $

Bread & Chocolate, 3.
5542 Connecticut Ave NW
☎ 966-7413. French. $

Busara, 32. 2340 Wisconsin Ave NW
☎ 337-2340. Thai. $

Cactus Cantina, 17.
3300 Wisconsin Ave NW
☎ 686-7222. Tex-Mex. $$

Cafe Deluxe, 19.
3228 Wisconsin Ave NW
☎ 686-2233. American. $$

Cafe Ole, 13. 4000 Wisconsin Ave NW
☎ 244-1330. Mediterranean. $

Caravela, 8. 4615 Wisconsin Ave NW
☎ 537-3200. Portugese. $$

Chadwick's, 3. 5247 Wisconsin Ave NW
☎ 362-8040. American. $$

Chef Geoff's, 12. 3201 New Mexico Ave
NW ☎ 237-7800. American. $$

Dancing Crab, 9.
4611 Wisconsin Ave NW
☎ 244-1882. Seafood. $$

Greenwood, 10.
5031 Connecticut Ave NW
☎ 364-4444. Vegetarian. $$$

Ireland's Four Provinces, 20.
3412 Connecticut Ave NW
☎ 244-0860. Irish. $$

Indique, 15. 3512-14 Connecticut Ave
NW ☎ 244-6600. Indian/Tapas. $$

Krupins Deli, 9.
4620 Wisconsin Ave NW ☎ 686-1989.
American. $$

Lavandou, 21. 3321 Connecticut Ave
NW ☎ 966-3002. French. $$

Lebanese Taverna, 24.
2641 Connecticut Ave NW
☎ 265-8681. Middle Eastern. $$

Maggiano's Little Italy, 1.
5333 Wisconsin Ave NW
☎ 966-5500. Italian $$

Mama Ayesha's, 26. 1967 Calvert St
NW ☎ 232-5431. Middle Eastern. $

New Heights, 25. 2317 Calvert St NW
☎ 234-4110. American. $$$

Old Europe, 29.
2434 Wisconsin Ave NW
☎ 333-7600. German. $$

Parthenon, 6.
5510 Connecticut Ave NW
☎ 966-7600. Greek. $$

Shanghai Garden, 13.
4469 Connecticut Ave NW
☎ 362-3000. Chinese. $

Sushi-Ko. 31. 2309 Wisconsin Ave NW
☎ 333-4187. Japanese. $$$

Thai Room, 11.
5037 Connecticut Ave NW
☎ 244-5933. Thai. $

Thai Town, 23. 2655 Connecticut Ave
NW ☎ 667-5115. Asian. $$

Trocadero Café, 27.
1914 Connecticut Ave NW
☎ 797-2000. French. $$$

2 Amys, 18. 3715 Macomb St NW
☎ 885-5700. Pizza. $$

Yanni's Greek Taverna, 16.
3500 Connecticut Ave NW
☎ 326-8871. Greek. $$

Yosaku, 7. 4712 Wisconsin Ave NW
☎ 363-4453. Japanese. $$

$$$$ = *over $35* $$$ = *$25-$35* $$ = *$15-$25* $ = *under $15*
Based on cost per person, excluding drinks, service, and 9% sales tax.

Listed Alphabetically

Air & Space Museum Cafeteria, 34.
Independence Ave & 6th St SW

**American History Museum
Cafeteria, 24.**
Madison Dr & 13th St NW

Armand's, 37. 226 Massachusetts NE

Bertucci's, 1.
2000 Pennsylvania Ave NW

Bread Line, 5.
1751 Pennsylvania Ave NW

Burger King, 8. 1606 K St NW

Cafe Mozart, 9. 1331 H St NW

Corcoran Gallery, 6. 500 17th St NW

Department of Agriculture, 28.
Independence Ave & 13th St SW

**Department of Health &
Human Services, 32.**
330 Independence Ave SW

**Department of Housing & Urban
Development, 30.** 451 7th St SW

Department of the Interior, 7.
1800 C St NW

Dirksen Senate Office Cafeteria, 40.
Constitution Ave & First St NE

Federal Trade Commission, 23.
Pennsylvania Ave & 6th St NW

Hard Rock Cafe, 21. 999 E St NW

Hirshhorn Outdoor Cafe, 33.
Independence Ave & 7th St SW

Holocaust Memorial Museum Cafe, 27.
200 Raoul Wallenberg Pl SW

Hotel Washington, 11.
515 15th St NW

International Sq. 2. 1850 K St NW

International Trade Center, 13.
E and 14th Sts NW

JW Marriott, 14. 1331 Penn Ave NW

Library of Congress Cafeteria, 38.
101 Independence Ave SE

Listed Alphabetically (cont.)

McDonald's, 3.
1101 Connecticut Ave NW

McDonald's, 31. 400 C St SW

National Aquarium Cafeteria, 12.
Constitution Ave & 14th St NW

National Gallery of Art Cafeteria, 26.
Constitution Ave & 6th St NW

**National Portrait Gallery
Cafeteria, 22.** F & 8th Sts NW

**Natural History Museum
Cafeteria, 25.** Madison Dr & 10th St NW

**New Executive Office Building
Cafeteria, 4.** H & 17th Sts NW

Old Ebbit Grill, 10.
675 15th St NW

Old Post Office Pavilion, 20.
1100 Pennsylvania Ave NW

Ollie's Trolley, 17. 425 12th NW

**Rayburn House
Building Cafeteria, 35.**
Independence Ave & First St SW

Shops at National Place, 15.
1331 Pennsylvania Ave NW

Skyline Cafe, 16. 1250 H St NW

**Smithsonian Castle,
"The Commons," 29.**
1000 Jefferson Dr SW

Supreme Court Cafeteria, 39.
1 First St NE

TGI Friday's, 19.
1201 Pennsylvania Ave NW

Union Station Pavilion, 36.
50 Massachusetts Ave NE

The Waffle Shop, 18.
522 10th St NW

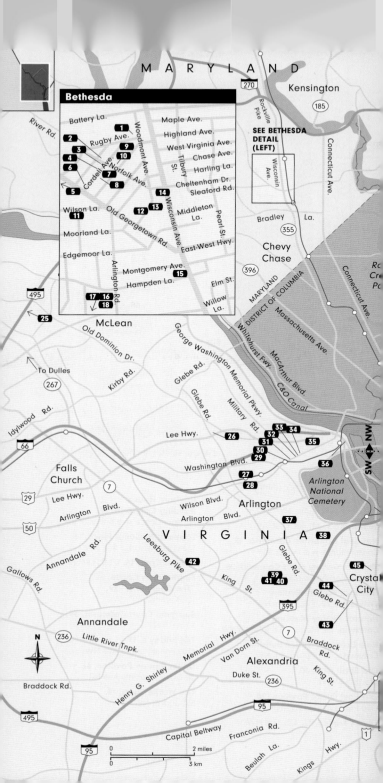

Listed by Site Number

1 Frascati
2 Bacchus-Bethesda
3 Tragara
4 La Panetteria
5 Jean-Michel
6 North China
7 Cottonwood Café
8 Matuba Bethesda
9 Tastee Diner
10 La Miche
11 Cafe Bethesda
12 Rio Grande
13 Haandi
14 Tako Grill
15 Pines of Rome
16 Raku
17 Thyme Square Cafe
18 Mon Ami Gabi
19 Golden Flame
20 Mrs K's Tollhouse
21 Negril
22 Crisfield
23 Langano
24 Cubano's
25 L'Auberge Chez Francois
26 Alpine
27 Rio Grande
28 Flat Top Grill
29 Aegean Taverna
30 Red, Hot & Blue
31 Pho 75
32 Whitlow's
33 Café Dalat
34 Queen Bee
35 Faccia Luna
36 Orleans House
37 Atilla's Restaurant
38 Bob & Edith's
39 Carlyle Grand
40 Bistro Bistro
41 Thai in Shirlington
42 Duangrat's
43 RT's
44 Portofino
45 Woo Lae Oak
46 Potowmack Landing
47 Tempo
48 Five Guys
49 Le Gaulois
50 Cafe Salsa
51 East Wind
52 South Austin Grill
53 Elysium
54 Taverna Cretekou
55 Bertucci's Brick Oven Pizza
56 Le Refuge
57 Geranio
58 King St Blues
59 La Madeleine
60 Gadsby's Tavern
61 Stardust
62 Bilbo Baggins
63 La Bergerie
64 Ecco Cafe
65 Chart House
66 Il Porto
67 The Wharf
68 Fish Market
69 Union Street Public House
70 Chadwicks
71 Blue Point Grill
72 Southside 815

BETHESDA, MD
Bacchus-Bethesda, 2.
7945 Norfolk Ave
☎ 301/657-1722. Lebanese. $$

Cafe Bethesda, 11. 5027 Wilson Lane
☎ 301/657-3383. American. $$

Cottonwood Café, 7. 4844 Cordell Ave
☎ 301/656-4844. American. $$

Frascati, 1. 4806 Rugby Ave
☎ 301/652-9514. Italian. $$

Haandi, 11. 4904 Fairmont Ave
☎ 301/718-0121. Indian. $

Jean-Michel, 5. 10223 Old G'town Rd
☎ 301/564-4910. French. $$

La Miche, 10. 7905 Norfolk Ave
☎ 301/986-0707. French. $$$

La Panetteria, 4. 4921 Cordell Ave
☎ 301/951-6433. Italian. $$

Matuba, 8. 4918 Cordell Ave
☎ 301/652-7449. Japanese. $$

Mon Ami Gabi, 18. 7239 Woodmont
Ave ☎ 301/654-1234. French. $$

North China, 6.
7814 Old Georgetown Rd
☎ 301/656-7922. Chinese. $

Pines of Rome, 15. 4709 Hampden La
☎ 301/657-8775. Italian. $$

Raku, 16. 7240 Woodmont
☎ 301/718-8680. Asian. $$

Rio Grande, 12. 4919 Fairmont Ave
☎ 301/656-2981. Tex-Mex. $$

Tako Grill, 14. 7756 Wisconsin Ave
☎ 301/652-7030. Japanese. $$

Tastee Diner, 9. 7731 Woodmont Ave
☎ 301/652-3970. American. $

Thyme Square Cafe, 17.
4735 Bethesda Ave ☎ 301/657-9077.
Vegetarian. $$

Tragara, 3. 4935 Cordell Ave
☎ 301/951-4935. Italian. $$$

SILVER SPRING, MD
Crisfield, 22. 8012 Georgia Ave
☎ 301/589-1306. Seafood. $$

Cubano's, 24. 1201 Fidler Lane
☎ 301/563-4020. Cuban. $$

Golden Flame, 19. 8630 Fenton St
☎ 301/588-7250. Continental. $$

Langano, 23. 8305 Georgia Ave
☎ 301/563-6700. Ethiopian. $

Mrs K's Tollhouse, 20.
9201 Colesville Rd ☎ 301/589-3500.
American. $$

Negril: The Jamaican Bakery &
Eatery, 21. 965 Thayer Ave
☎ 301/585-3000. Jamaican. $$

GREAT FALLS, VA
L'Auberge Chez Francois, 25.
332 Springvale Rd ☎ 703/759-3800.
French. $$$$

ARLINGTON, VA
Aegean Taverna, 29.
2950 Clarendon Blvd
☎ 703/841-9494. Greek. $$

Alpine, 26. 4770 Lee Hwy
☎ 703/528-7600. Italian. $$

Atilla's Restaurant, 37.
2705 Columbia Pike ☎ 703/920-8100.
Middle Eastern. $$

Bistro Bistro, 40. 4021 S. 28th St
☎ 703/379-0300. American. $$

Bob & Edith's Diner, 38.
2310 Columbia Pike ☎ 703/920-6103.
Diner. $

Cafe Dalat, 33. 3143 Wilson Blvd
☎ 703/276-0935. Vietnamese. $$

Carlyle Grand, 39. 4000 S 28th St
☎ 703/931-0777. American. $$

Duangrat's, 42. 5878 Leesburg Pike
☎ 703/820-5775. Thai. $$

Faccia Luna, 35. 2909 Wilson Blvd
☎ 703/276-3099. Italian. $$

Flat Top Grill, 28. 4245 N Fairfax
☎ 703/578-0078. Stir-fry. $$

Little Viet Garden, 31. 3012 Wilson Blvd
☎ 703/522-9686. Vietnamese. $$

Orleans House, 36. 1213 Wilson Blvd
☎ 703/524-2929. American. $$

Pho 75, 31. 1721 Wilson Blvd
☎ 703/525-7355. Vietnamese. $

Portofino, 44. 526 S 23rd St
☎ 703/979-8200. Italian. $$

Queen Bee, 34. 3181 Wilson Blvd
☎ 703/527-3444. Vietnamese. $

RT's, 43. 3804 Mt Vernon St
☎ 703/684-6010. Seafood. $$

Red, Hot & Blue, 30. 1600 Wilson Blvd
☎ 703/276-7427. Southern/BBQ. $$

Rio Grande, 27. 4301 N Fairfax Dr
☎ 703/528-3131. Tex-Mex. $$

Thai in Shirlington, 41. 4029 S 28th St
☎ 703/931-3203. Thai. $$

Whitlow's on Wilson, 32. 2854
Wilson Blvd ☎ 703/276-9693. Diner. $

Listed Alphabetically (cont.)

Woo Lae Oak, 45. 1500 S. Joyce St
☎ 703/521-3706. Korean. $

ALEXANDRIA, VA

Bertucci's Brick Oven Pizza, 55.
725 King St ☎ 703/548-0500. Italian. $

Bilbo Baggins, 62. 208 Queen St
☎ 703/683-0300. American. $$

Blue Point Grill, 71. 600 Franklin St
☎ 703/739-0404. Seafood. $$$

Cafe Salsa, 50. 808 King St
☎ 703/684-4100. Latin American. $$

Chadwick's, 70. 203 S. Strand St
☎ 703/836-4442. American. $$

Chart House, 65. 1 Cameron St
☎ 703/684-5080. Seafood. $$$

East Wind, 51. 809 King St
☎ 703/836-1515. Vietnamese. $$

Ecco Cafe, 64. 220 N Lee
☎ 703/684-0321. Italian. $$

Elysium, 53. 116 S Alfred St
☎ 703/838-8000. American. $$$

Fish Market, 68. 105 King St
☎ 703/836-5676. Seafood. $

Five Guys, 48. 107 N Fayette St
☎ 703/549-7991. Burgers. $

Gadsby's Tavern, 60. 138 N Royal St
☎ 703/548-1288. American. $$$

Geranio, 57. 722 King St
☎ 703/548-0088. Italian. $$

Il Porto, 66. 121 King St
☎ 703/836-8833. Italian. $$

King St Blues, 58. 112 N St Asaph St
☎ 703/836-8800. Downhome. $

La Bergerie, 63. 218 N Lee St
☎ 703/683-1007. French. $$$$

Le Gaulois, 49. 1106 King St
☎ 703/739-9494. French. $$

La Madeleine, 59. 500 King St
☎ 703/739-2854. Bakery/Cafe. $

Le Refuge, 56. 127 N Washington St
☎ 703/548-4661. French. $$

Potowmack Landing, 46. 1 Marina Dr
☎ 703/548-0001. Seafood. $$$

South Austin Grill, 52. 801 King St
☎ 703/684-8969. Tex-Mex. $

Southside 815, 72. 815 S Washington St
☎ 703/836-6222. American. $$

Stardust, 61. 608 Montgomery
☎ 703/548-9864. Fusion. $$

Taverna Cretekou, 54. 818 King St
☎ 703/548-8688. Greek. $$

Tempo, 47. 4231 Duke St
☎ 703/370-7900. Italian. $$

Union St Public House, 69.
121 S Union St ☎ 703/548-1785.
American. $$

The Wharf, 70. 119 King St
☎ 703/836-2834. Seafood. $$$

$$$$ = over $35 $$$ = $25-$35 $$ = $15-$25 $ = under $15
Based on cost per person, excluding drinks, service, and 9% sales tax in DC, 4.5% in VA, and 5% in MD

Listed by Site Number

1 Holiday Inn-
   Georgetown
2 Savoy Suites
3 Days Inn-Uptown
4 Kalorama-Woodley
5 Omni Shoreham
6 Marriott Wardman-
   Park
7 Kalorama-Kalorama
   Park
8 Adams Inn
9 Windsor Park
10 Normandy Inn
11 Churchill Hotel
12 Washington
   Courtyard by
   Marriott

13 Washington Hilton
   and Towers
14 Carlyle Suites
15 Windsor Inn
16 Embassy Inn
17 Hilton Washington
   Embassy Row
18 Radisson Barcelo
19 Westin Embassy Row
20 Georgetown Inn
21 Latham
22 Four Seasons
23 Washington Suites
   Georgetown
24 The Melrose
   of Washington
25 River Inn

26 George Washington
   University Inn
27 Watergate
28 Doubletree Guest
   Suites
29 Lombardy
30 One Washington Cir
31 The Westin Grand
32 Park Hyatt
33 Fairmont
   Washington
34 Embassy Suites
35 Washington Marriott
36 Sheraton City Centre
37 Lincoln Suites
38 Embassy Square
   Suites

Listed by Site Number (cont.)

39 Hotel Madera

40 Tabard Inn

41 The Topaz

42 Governors House

43 Hotel Rouge

44 Washington Terrace Hotel

45 Holiday Inn-Central

46 Hotel Helix

47 Jefferson

48 Mayflower

49 Madison

50 Wyndham Washington

51 Washington Plaza

52 Holiday Inn Downtown

53 Hamilton Crowne Plaza

54 Morrison-Clark Inn

55 AYH Hostel

56 Henley Park

57 Howard Johnson Express Inn

58 Capital Hilton

59 St Regis

60 Hay-Adams

61 Hotel Washington

62 Willard Inter-Continental

63 JW Marriott

64 Harrington

65 Marriott Metro Center

66 Grand Hyatt

67 Washington Renaissance

68 Red Roof Inn-DC

69 Super 8

70 Washington Court

71 Phoenix Park

72 Hotel George

73 Hyatt Regency

74 Holiday Inn on the Hill

75 Holiday Inn-Capitol

76 Capitol Hill Suites

77 Channel Inn

78 Loew's L'Enfant Plaza

79 Best Western Capital Skyline

Listed Alphabetically

Adams Inn, 8. 1744 Lanier Pl NW
☎ 745-3600. 🖷 319-7958. $

AYH Hostel, 55. 1009 11th St NW
☎ 737-2333. 🖷 737-1508. $

Capital Hilton, 58. 1001 16th St NW
☎ 393-1000. 🖷 639-5784. $$$$

Best Western Capital Skyline, 79.
10 I St SW ☎ 488-7500. 🖷 488-0790. $

Capitol Hill Suites, 76. 200 C St SE
☎ 543-6000. 🖷 547-2608. $$

Carlyle Suites, 14.
1731 New Hampshire Ave NW
☎ 234-3200. 🖷 387-0085. $

Channel Inn, 77. 650 Water St SW
☎ 554-2400. 🖷 863-1164. $

Churchill Hotel, 11. 1914 Connecticut
Ave NW ☎ 797-2000. 🖷 462-0944.
$$$

Days Inn-Uptown, 3.
4400 Connecticut Ave NW
☎ 244-5600. 🖷 244-6794. $

Doubletree Guest Suites, 28.
801 New Hampshire Ave NW
☎ 785-2000. 🖷 785-9485. $$

Embassy Inn, 16. 1627 16th St NW
☎ 234-7800. 🖷 234-3309. $

Embassy Square Suites, 38.
2000 N St NW
☎ 659-9000. 🖷 429-9546. $$

Embassy Suites, 34. 1250 22nd St NW
☎ 857-3388. 🖷 293-3173. $$$

Fairmont Washington, 33. 2401 M St
NW ☎ 429-2400. 🖷 457-5010. $$$$

Four Seasons, 22. 2800 Penn Ave
NW ☎ 342-0444. 🖷 944-2032. $$$$

**George Washington University
Inn, 26.** 824 New Hampshire Ave NW
☎ 337-6620. 🖷 298-7499. $$

Georgetown Inn, 20.
1310 Wisconsin Ave NW
☎ 333-8900. 🖷 333-8308. $$

Governors House, 42.
1615 Rhode Island Ave NW
☎ 296-2100. 🖷 331-0227. $

Grand Hyatt, 66. 1000 H St NW
☎ 582-1234. 🖷 637-4781. $$$

Hamilton Crowne Plaza, 53.
1001 14th St NW
☎ 682-0111. 🖷 682-9525. $$$

Harrington, 64. 436 11th St NW
☎ 628-8140. 🖷 347-3924. $

Hay-Adams, 60. 800 16th St NW
☎ 638-6600. 🖷 638-2716. $$$$

Henley Park, 56.
926 Massachusetts Ave NW
☎ 638-5200. 🖷 638-6740. $$$

Hilton Washington Embassy Row, 17.
2015 Mass Ave NW
☎ 265-1600. 🖷 328-7526. $$$

Holiday Inn on the Hill, 74.
415 New Jersey Ave NW
☎ 638-1616. 🖷 638-0707. $$

Holiday Inn-Capitol, 75. 550 C St SW
☎ 479-4000. 🖷 479-4353. $$

Holiday Inn-Central, 45.
1501 Rhode Island Ave NW
☎ 483-2000. 🖷 797-1078. $

Holiday Inn Downtown, 52.
1155 14th St NW
☎ 737-1200. 🖷 783-5733. $$

Holiday Inn-Georgetown, 1.
2101 Wisconsin Ave NW
☎ 338-4600. 🖷 338-4458. $$

Hotel George, 72. 15 E St NW
☎ 347-4200. 🖷 347-4213. $$$$

Hotel Helix, 46.
1430 Rhode Island Ave NW
☎ 462-7777. 🖷 332-3519. $

Hotel Madera, 39.
1310 New Hampshire Ave NW
☎ 296-7600. 🖷 293-2476. $$

Hotel Rouge, 43. 1315 16th St NW
☎ 232-8000. 🖷 667-9827. $$

Hotel Washington, 61. 515 15th St NW
☎ 638-5900. 🖷 638-4275. $$$

Howard Johnson Express Inn, 57.
600 New York Ave NE
☎ 546-9200. 🖷 546-6348. $

Hyatt Regency, 73.
400 New Jersey Ave NW
☎ 737-1234. 🖷 737-5773. $$$$

Jefferson, 47. 1200 16th St NW
☎ 347-2200. 🖷 223-9039. $$$$

JW Marriott, 63. 1331 Penn Ave NW
☎ 393-2000. 🖷 626-6991. $$$$

**Kalorama Guesthouse at Kalorama
Park, 7.** 1854 Mintwood Pl NW
☎ 667-6369. 🖷 319-1262. $

**Kalorama Guesthouse at Woodley
Park, 4.** 2700 Cathedral Ave NW
☎ 328-0860. 🖷 328-8730. $

Latham, 21. 3000 M St NW
☎ 726-5000. 🖷 337-4250. $$

Lincoln Suites, 37. 1823 L St NW
☎ 223-4320. 🖷 223-8546. $$$

oew's L'Enfant Plaza, 78.
▪80 L'Enfant Plaza SW
☎ 484–1000. 🖷646–4456. $$$

ombardy, 29.
▪019 Pennsylvania Ave NW
☎ 828–2600. 🖷872–0503. $$

Madison, 49. 1177 15th St NW
☎ 862–1600. 🖷785–1255. $$$$

Marriott Metro Center, 65.
▪75 12th St NW
☎ 737–2200. 🖷347–5886. $$

Marriott Wardman-Park, 6.
▪660 Woodley Rd NW
☎ 328–2000. 🖷234–0015. $$$

Mayflower, 48. 1127 Connecticut Ave NW
☎ 347–3000. 🖷776–9182. $$$$

The Melrose of Washington, 24.
▪430 Pennsylvania Ave NW
☎ 955–6400. 🖷955–5765. $$$

Morrison-Clark Inn, 54. 1015 L St NW
☎ 898–1200. 🖷289–8576. $$$

Normandy Inn, 10. 2118 Wyoming Ave
NW ☎ 483–1350. 🖷387–8241. $

Omni Shoreham, 5. 2500 Calvert St NW
☎ 234–0700. 🖷265–7962. $$$$

One Washington Circle, 30.
▪ Washington Circle NW
☎ 872–1680. 🖷887–4989. $$

Park Hyatt, 31. 1201 24th St NW
☎ 789–1234. 🖷419–6795. $$$$

Phoenix Park, 71. 520 N Capitol St NW
☎ 638–6900. 🖷393–3236. $$

Radisson Barcelo, 18. 2121 P St NW
☎ 293–3100. 🖷857–0134. $$$

Red Roof Inn-DC, 68. 500 H St NW
☎ 289–5959. 🖷682–9152. $

River Inn, 25. 924 25th St NW
☎ 337–7600. 🖷337–6520. $$$

Savoy Suites, 2. 2505 Wisconsin Ave
NW ☎ 337–9700. 🖷337–3644. $$

Sheraton City Centre, 36.
1143 New Hampshire Ave NW
☎ 775–0800. 🖷331–9491. $$$

St Regis, 59. 923 16th St NW
☎ 638–2626. 🖷638–4231. $$$$

Super 8 Washington, 69.
501 New York Ave NE
☎ 543–7400. 🖷544–2327. $

Tabard Inn, 40. 1733 N St NW
☎ 785–1277. 🖷785–6173. $$

The Topaz, 41. 1739 N St NW
☎ 393–3000. 🖷785–9581. $$

Washington Court, 70.
525 New Jersey Ave NW
☎ 628–2100. 🖷879–7918. $$$

**Washington Courtyard by Marriott,
12.** 1900 Connecticut Ave NW
☎ 332–9300. 🖷328–7039. $$

Washington Hilton and Towers, 13.
1919 Connecticut Ave NW
☎ 483–3000. 🖷232–0438. $$$$

Washington Marriott, 35.
1221 22nd St NW
☎ 872–1500. 🖷872–1424. $$$$

Washington Plaza, 51. 10 Thomas Cir
NW ☎ 842–1300. 🖷371–9602. $$$

Washington Renaissance, 67.
999 9th St NW
☎ 898–9000. 🖷289–0947. $$$

Washington Suites Georgetown, 23.
2500 Pennsylvania Ave NW
☎ 333–8060. 🖷338–3818. $$$

Washington Terrace Hotel, 44.
1515 Rhode Island Ave NW
☎ 232–7000. 🖷521–7103. $$

Watergate, 27. 2650 Virginia Ave NW
☎ 965–2300. 🖷337–7915. $$$$

Westin Embassy Row, 19.
2100 Massachusetts Ave NW
☎ 293–2100. 🖷293–0641. $$$$

The Westin Grand, 31. 2350 M St NW
☎ 429–0100. 🖷429–9759. $$$$

Willard Inter-Continental, 62.
1401 Pennsylvania Ave NW
☎ 628–9100. 🖷637–7326. $$$$

Windsor Inn, 15. 1842 16th St NW
☎ 667–0300. 🖷667–4503. $

Windsor Park, 9. 2116 Kalorama Rd
NW ☎ 483–7700. 🖷332–4547. $

Wyndham Washington, 50.
1400 M St NW
☎ 429–1700. 🖷785–0786. $$$

$$$$ = *over $215* $$$ = *$155-$215* $$ = *$125-$155* $ = *under $125*
*All prices are for a standard double room, excluding 10% room tax, and are
weekday rates; weekend rates are often reduced.*

Listed by Site Number

ROCKVILLE, MD

1 Courtyard by Marriott
2 Quality Suites
3 Best Western
4 Doubletree

BETHESDA, MD

5 Marriott
6 Four Points by Sheraton
7 Holiday Inn
8 American Inn
9 Hyatt Regency
10 Bethesda Court Hotel
11 Marriott Residence Inn

CHEVY CHASE, MD

12 Holiday Inn

SILVER SPRING, MD

13 Holiday Inn
14 Hilton
15 Courtyard by Marriott

COLLEGE PARK, MD

16 Holiday Inn
17 Quality Inn

DULLES INT'L AIRPORT, VA

18 Holiday Inn Dulles
19 Hyatt Dulles
20 Hilton Washington at Dulles

MCLEAN, VA

21 Hilton McLean
22 Best Western
23 Ritz-Carlton Tysons Corner
24 Holiday Inn-Tysons Corner

VIENNA, VA

25 Sheraton Premiere at Tysons Corner
26 Embassy Suites
27 Marriott

FALLS CHURCH, VA

28 Doubletree
29 Quality Inn-Governor
30 Comfort Inn-Washington Gateway West

ARLINGTON, VA

31 Arlington Hilton and Towers
32 Holiday Inn-Arlington
33 Quality Inn
34 Holiday Inn-Rosslyn
35 Hyatt Arlington
36 Marriott-Key Bridge
37 Econo Lodge-Pentagon
38 Sheraton National
39 Doubletree Crystal City
40 Embassy Suites
41 Crowne Plaza
42 Marriott-Crystal Gateway
43 Ritz-Carlton Pentagon City
44 Sheraton Crystal
45 Crystal City Marriott
46 Hilton Crystal City
47 Hyatt Regency
48 Holiday Inn

ALEXANDRIA, VA

49 Radisson
50 Holiday Inn Suites
51 Morrison House
52 Holiday Inn-Old Town
53 Hilton Alexandria Old Town
54 Residence Inn Alexandria Old Town
55 Embassy Suites Hotel Alexandria
56 Travelers Motel
57 Hilton Alexandria
58 Days Inn Alexandria
59 Washington Suites Alexandria

Listed Alphabetically

BETHESDA, MD

American Inn, 8.
8130 Wisconsin Ave
☎ 301/656-9300. 🖷 656-2907. $

Bethesda Court Hotel, 10.
7740 Wisconsin Ave ☎ 301/656-2100.
🖷 986-0375. $$

Four Points by Sheraton, 6.
8400 Wisconsin Ave ☎ 301/718-0679.
🖷 986-1715. $$

Holiday Inn, 7. 8120 Wisconsin Ave
☎ 301/652-2000. 🖷 652-4525. $$

Hyatt Regency, 9. 7400 Wisconsin Ave
☎ 301/657-1234. 🖷 657-6453. $$$

Marriott, 5. 5151 Pooks Hill Rd
☎ 301/897-9400. 🖷 897-0192. $$$

**Marriott Residence Inn, Bethesda
Downtown, 11.** 7335 Wisconsin Ave
☎ 301/718-0200. 🖷 913-0197. $$

CHEVY CHASE, MD

Holiday Inn, 12. 5520 Wisconsin Ave
☎ 301/656-1500. 🖷 656-5045. $$

COLLEGE PARK, MD

Holiday Inn, 16.
10,000 Baltimore Ave
☎ 301/345-6700. 🖷 441-4923. $

Quality Inn, 17. 7200 Baltimore Ave
☎ 301/864-5820. 🖷 927-8634. $

ROCKVILLE, MD

Best Western, 3
1251 W Montgomery Ave
☎ 301/424-4940. 🖷 424-1047. $

Courtyard by Marriott, 1.
2500 Research Blvd ☎ 301/670-6700.
🖷 670-9023. $

Doubletree, 4. 1750 Rockville Pike
☎ 301/468-1100. 🖷 468-0163. $$

Quality Suites, 2. 3 Research Court
☎ 301/840-0200. 🖷 258-0160. $

SILVER SPRING, MD

Courtyard by Marriott, 15.
12521 Prosperity Dr ☎ 301/680-8500.
🖷 680-9232. $

**Hilton Washington DC
Silver Spring, 14.** 8727 Colesville Rd
☎ 301/589-5200. 🖷 563-3832. $

Holiday Inn, 13. 8777 Georgia Ave
☎ 301/589-0800. 🖷 587-4791. $

ALEXANDRIA, VA

Days Inn Alexandria, 58.
110 S Bragg St ☎ 703/354-4950.
🖷 642-2873. $

**Embassy Suites Hotel Alexandria-
Old Town, 55.** 1900 Diagonal Rd
☎ 703/684-5900. 🖷 684-1403. $$$

Hilton Alexandria Mark Center, 57.
5000 Seminary Rd ☎ 703/845-1010.
🖷 845-7662. $$

Hilton Alexandria Old Town, 53.
1767 King St ☎ 703/837-0440.
🖷 703/837-0454. $$$

Holiday Inn-Old Town, 52.
480 King St ☎ 703/549-6080.
🖷 684-6508. $$$

Holiday Inn Suites, 50. 625 First St
☎ 703/548-6300. 🖷 548-8032. $

Morrison House, 51. 116 S Alfred St
☎ 703/838-8000. 🖷 684-6283. $$$

Radisson, 49. 901 N Fairfax St
☎ 703/683-6000. 🖷 683-7597. $

**Residence Inn Alexandria
Old Town, 54.** 1456 Duke St
☎ 703/548-5474. 🖷 684-6818. $$

Travelers Motel, 56.
5916 Richmond Hwy ☎ 703/329-1310.
🖷 960-9211. $

Washington Suites Alexandria, 59.
100 S Reynolds St ☎ 703/370-9600.
🖷 370-0467. $$

ARLINGTON, VA

Arlington Hilton and Towers, 31.
950 N Stafford St ☎ 703/528-6000.
🖷 528-4386. $$

Crowne Plaza National Airport, 41.
1489 Jefferson Davis Hwy
☎ 703/416-1600. 🖷 416-1615. $$

Crystal City Marriott, 45.
1999 Jefferson Davis Hwy
☎ 703/413-5500. 🖷 413-0192. $$$

Doubletree Crystal City , 39.
300 Army-Navy Dr ☎ 703/416-4100.
🖷 416-4126. $$

Econo Lodge-Pentagon, 37.
5666 Columbia Pike ☎ 703/820-5600
🖷 379-7482. $

Embassy Suites Crystal City, 40.
1300 Jefferson Davis Hwy
☎ 703/979-9799. 🖷 920-5947. $$$$

Hilton Crystal City, 46.
2399 Jefferson Davis Hwy
☎ 703/418-6800. 🖷 418-3763. $$$

Holiday Inn-Arlington, 32.
4610 N. Fairfax ☎ 703/243-9800.
📠 527-2677. $$$

Holiday Inn-Rosslyn, 34.
1900 N Ft Meyer Dr
☎ 703/807-2006. 📠 522-8864. $$

Holiday Inn, 48.
2650 Jefferson Davis Hwy
☎ 703/684-7200. 📠 684-3217. $$$

Hyatt Arlington, 35. 1325 Wilson Blvd
☎ 703/525-1234. 📠 908-4790. $$$

Hyatt Regency Crystal City, 47.
2799 Jefferson Davis Hwy
☎ 703/418-1234. 📠 418-1289. $$$

Marriott-Crystal Gateway, 42.
1700 Jefferson Davis Hwy
☎ 703/920-3230. 📠 271-5212. $$$

Marriott-Key Bridge, 36. 1401 Lee Hwy
☎ 703/524-6400. 📠 524-8964. $$

Quality Suites-Courthouse Plaza, 33.
1200 N Courthouse Rd
☎ 703/524-4000. 📠 522-6814. $

Ritz-Carlton Pentagon City, 43.
1250 S Hayes St ☎ 703/415-5000.
📠 415-5061. $$$$

Sheraton Crystal City, 44.
1800 Jefferson Davis Hwy
☎ 703/486-1111. 📠 769-3970. $$

Sheraton National, 38.
900 S Orme St ☎ 703/521-1900.
📠 271-6626 $$

DULLES INTERNATIONAL AIRPORT, VA

Hilton Washington Dulles, 20.
13869 Park Center Rd, Herndon
☎ 703/478-2900. 📠 834-1996. $$

Holiday Inn Dulles, 18.
1000 Sully Rd, Sterling
☎ 703/471-7411. 📠 834-7558. $$$

Hyatt Dulles, 19.
2300 Dulles Corner Blvd, Herndon
☎ 703/713-1234. 📠 713-3410. $$

FALLS CHURCH, VA

Comfort Inn-Washington Gateway West, 30.
6111 Arlington Blvd ☎ 703/534-9100.
📠 534-5589. $

Doubletree at Tyson's Corner, 28.
7801 Leesburg Pike ☎ 703/893-1340.
📠 847-9520. $$

Quality Inn-Governor, 29.
6650 Arlington Blvd ☎ 703/532-8900.
📠 532-7121. $

MCLEAN, VA

Best Western Tyson's Westpark Hotel, 22. 8401 Westpark Dr
☎ 703/734-2800. 📠 821-8872. $$

Hilton McLean / Tyson's Corner, 21.
7920 Jones Branch Dr
☎ 703/847-5000. 📠 761-5100. $$$

Holiday Inn-Tysons Corner, 24.
1960 Chain Bridge Road
☎ 703/893-2100. 📠 356-8218. $$

Ritz-Carlton Tysons Corner, 23.
1700 Tysons Blvd ☎ 703/506-4300.
📠 506-2694. $$$$

VIENNA, VA

Embassy Suites, 26.
8517 Leesburg Pike ☎ 703/883-0707.
📠 883-0694. $$$

Marriott at Tysons Corner, 27.
8028 Leesburg Pike ☎ 703/734-3200.
📠 734-5763. $$$

Sheraton Premiere at Tysons Corner, 25.
8661 Leesburg Pike ☎ 703/448-1234.
📠 610-8293. $$

$$$$ = over $215 $$$ = $155-$215 $$ = $125-$155 $ = under $100
All prices are for a standard double room, excluding 10% room tax, and are weekday rates; weekend rates are often reduced.

Listed by Site Number

1	Adventure Theatre	**5**	Carter Barron Amph	**12**	Duke Ellington Theatre
1	Imagination Stage	**6**	Source Theatre Co	**13**	Scena Theatre
1	Round House Theatre	**6**	Wash Stage Guild	**14**	Joy of Motion
2	Black Rock Center	**7**	Lincoln Theater	**15**	Church St Theatre
3	DC/AC	**8**	Olney Theatre	**16**	Theater J
3	Theatre Conspiracy	**9**	Cramton Aud	**17**	Studio Theatre
4	Washington Storytellers Theatre	**10**	Dance Place	**18**	Gallaudet Theatre
		11	Hartke Theatre	**19**	Wolf Trap-The Barns

Listed Alphabetically

Adventure Theatre, 1. 7300 MacArthur Blvd, Glen Echo, MD ☎ 301/320-5331

Arena Stage, 40. Maine Ave & 6th St SW ☎ 488-3300

Baird Auditorium, 33. Nat'l Mus of Natural History, Constitution Ave & 10th St NW ☎ 357-1650

Black Rock Center for the Performing Arts, 2. 12901 Town Commons Dr, Germantown, MD ☎ 301/508-2260

Carmichael Auditorium, 32. Nat'l Mus of American History, Constitution Ave & 14th St NW ☎ 357-2700

Carter Barron Amphitheatre, 5. Colorado Ave & 16th St NW ☎ 426-0486

Church St Theatre, 15. 1742 Church St NW ☎ 265-3748

Constitution Hall, 25. 18th & D Sts NW ☎ 628-2661

Cramton Auditorium, 9. Howard Univ, 2455 6th St NW ☎ 806-7198

Dance Place, 10. 3225 8th St NE ☎ 269-1600

DC/AC, 3. 2438 18th St NW ☎ 462-7833

Discovery Theatre, 36. 900 Jefferson Dr SW ☎ 357-1500

Duke Ellington Theatre, 12. 3500 R St NW ☎ 342-7589

Folger Elizabethan Theatre, 35. 201 E Capitol St SE ☎ 544-7077

Ford's Theatre, 28. 511 10th St NW ☎ 638-2941

GALA Hispanic Theater, 29. 1021 7th St NW ☎ 234-7174

Gallaudet Theatre, 18. 800 Florida Ave NE ☎ 651-5500

Hammer Auditorium, 24. Corcoran Gallery, New York Ave & 17th St NW ☎ 639-1700

Hartke Theatre, 11. Catholic Univ, 3801 Harewood Rd NE ☎ 319-4000

Imagination Stage, 1. 4908 Auburn Ave, Bethesda, MD ☎ 301/280-1660

Improv, 21. 1140 Connecticut Ave NW ☎ 296-7008

The John Fitzgerald Kennedy Center for the Performing Arts, 23. 2700 F St NW ☎ 467-4600

Joy of Motion Dance Place, 14. 1643 Connecticut Ave NW ☎ 387-0911

Lincoln Theater, 7. 1215 U St NW ☎ 328-6000

Lisner Auditorium, 22. 21st & H Sts NW ☎ 994-1500

MCI Center, 30. 601 F St NW ☎ 628-3200

Metro Stage, 38. 1201 N. Royal St., Alexandria, VA ☎ 703/548-9044

National Gallery of Art, 34. Constitution Ave & 6th St NW ☎ 737-4215

National Theatre, 26. 1321 Pennsylvania Ave NW ☎ 628-6161

Nissan Pavilion, 39. 7800 Cellar Door Dr, Bristow, VA ☎ 703/754-6400

Olney Theatre, 8. 2001 Olney-Sandy Spring Rd, Olney, MD ☎ 301/924-3400

Round House Theatre, 1. 7501 Wisconsin Ave, Bethesda MD ☎ 240/644-1100

Scena Theatre, 13. 1614 19th St NW ☎ 684-7990

Shakespeare at the Lansburgh, 31. 450 7th St NW ☎ 547-1122

Signature Theater, 38. 3806 Four Mile Run, Arlington, VA ☎ 703/218-6500

Source Theatre Co, 6. 1835 14th St NW ☎ 462-1073

Studio Theatre, 17. 1333 P St NW ☎ 332-3300

Sylvan Theatre, 37. Washington Monument Grounds ☎ 619-7222

Theatre J, 16. 1529 16th St NW ☎ 800/494-8497

The Theatre Conspiracy, 3. 2438 18th St NW ☎ 466-1629

Theatre of the First Amendment George Mason University, 20. Fairfax, VA ☎ 703/993-3000

Warehouse Theatre, 29. 1021 7th St NW ☎ 783-3933

Warner Theatre, 27. 513 13th St NW ☎ 783-4000

Washington Shakespeare Company, 38. 601 S. Clark St., Arlington, VA ☎ 703/418-4808

Washington Stage Guild, 28. 1901 14th St NW ☎ 240/582-0050

Washington Storytellers Theatre, 4. 7050 Carroll Ave, Takoma Park, MD ☎ 301/891-1129

Wolf Trap-The Barns, 19. 1635 Trap Rd, Vienna, VA ☎ 703/938-2404

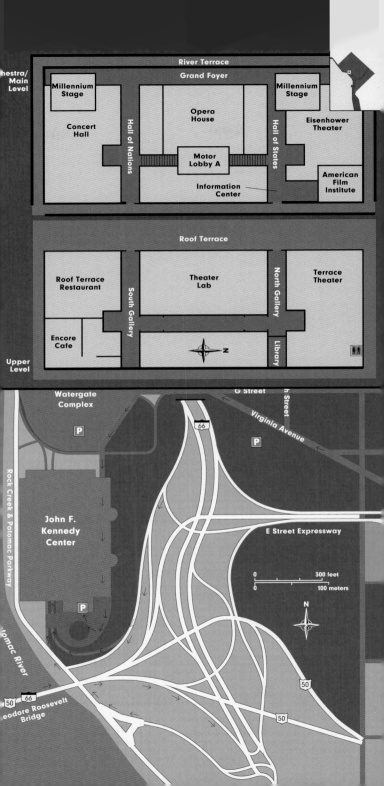

Listed by Site Number

1 Avalon Theater
2 Landmark's Bethesda Row
3 United Artists Bethesda
4 Cineplex Odeon Cinema
5 Outer Circle
6 Mazza Gallerie
7 Wisconsin Ave
8 Uptown
9 AFI Silver Theatre & Cultural Center
10 AMC Academy 8
11 Regal Bowie Stadium Fourteen
12 Visions Cinema Bistro Lounge
13 Dupont Circle V
14 Loew's Georgetown
15 American Film Institute
16 Inner Circle

Listed Alphabetically

AFI Silver Theatre & Cultural Center, 9. 8633 Colesville Rd, Silver Spring ☎ 301/495-6700

AMC Academy 8, 10. Beltway Plaza Mall, Greenbelt, MD ☎ 703/998-4262

AMC Courthouse, 23. 2150 Clarendon Blvd, Arlington ☎ 703/998-4262

AMC Mazza Gallerie, 6. 5300 Wisconsin Ave NW, 3rd Floor ☎ 357-9553

AMC Union Station IX, 18. 50 Massachusetts Ave ☎ 703/998-4262

American Film Institute Theater, 15. Kennedy Center, 2700 F St NW ☎ 785-4600

Arlington Cinema 'n' Drafthouse, 21. 2903 Columbia Pike ☎ 703/486-2345

Avalon Theater, 1. 5612 Connecticut Ave NW ☎ 966-6000

Cinema Arts Theater, 24. Rte 236 W & Pickett Rd, Fairfax ☎ 703/978-6991

Cineplex Odeon Cinema, 4. 5100 Wisconsin Ave NW ☎ 966-7248

Cineplex Loew's Dupont Circle V, 13. 1350 19th St NW ☎ 872-9555

Cineplex Odeon Inner Circle, 16. 2301 M St NW ☎ 333-3456

Cineplex Odeon Outer Circle, 5. 4849 Wisconson Ave NW ☎ 244-3166

Cineplex Odeon Shirlington Seven, 22. 2772 S Randolph St, Arlington, VA ☎ 703/671-0978

Listed by Site Number (cont.)

17 Samuel C. Johnson IMAX Theater

18 AMC Union Station IX

19 National Air & Space Lockheed Martin IMAX Theatre

20 Hoyt's Potomac Yards

21 Arlington Cinema 'n' Drafthouse

22 Shirlington

23 AMC Courthouse

24 Cinema Arts Theater

Listed Alphabetically (cont.)

Cineplex Odeon Uptown, 8.
3426 Connecticut Ave NW
☎ 966–5400

Cineplex Odeon Wisconsin, 7.
4000 Wisconsin Ave NW ☎ 244–0880

Hoyt's Potomac Yards, 20
3575 Jefferson Davis Highway, VA
☎ 703/739–4040

Landmark's Bethesda Row, 2.
7235 Woodmont Ave ☎ 301/652–7273

Loew's Georgetown, 14. 3111 K St NW
☎ 274–1728

National Air & Space Lockheed Martin IMAX Theatre, 19.
6th St & Independence Aves SW
☎ 357–1686

Regal Bowie Stadium Fourteen, 11.
15200 Major Lansdale Blvd
☎ 301/262–7433

Samuel C. Johnson IMAX Theater, 17.
National Museum of Natural History
10th & Constitution NW ☎ 633–7400

United Artists Bethesda, 3
7272 Wisconsin Ave ☎ 301/718–4323

Visions Cinema Bistro Lounge, 12.
1927 Florida Ave NW ☎ 667–0090

MAP **57** **Nightlife/Washington**